mBIT Coaching Workbook

Facilitators Guide

"Coaching clients' head, heart and gut intelligences to evolve their world"

*m*BIT (multiple Brain Integration Techniques) Coaching is a rapidly growing new field. There are now Coaches and Trainers across the planet. All of whom are making transformational and profound differences to their Clients' lives using *m*BIT.

Incorporating leading edge methodologies and the latest neuroscience findings, the *m*BIT Coaching Workbook provides a powerful system for supporting, communicating with and integrating the wisdom and intelligence of your Clients' multiple brains. This *Facilitators Guide* for the mBIT Coaching Workbook teaches you how to best utilize the exercises with your Clients to facilitate them up the *m*BIT Roadmap – using the *m*BIT Roadmap as a developmental competency hierarchy.

By using the exercises in the *m*BIT Coaching Workbook, you can deeply amplify your Clients' personal evolution and help them achieve even greater success and happiness in a world of massive change. With this *m*BIT Coaching Workbook you can truly evolve your Clients' multiple brains and their world!

mBIT Coaching Workbook

Facilitators Guide

GRANT SOOSALU AND MARVIN OKA

www.mbraining.com

Copyright © 2014 mBIT International Pty Ltd

ISBN 978-1495938535

All rights reserved. No part of this publication may be reproduced, stored in a retrieval system, or transmitted in any form or by any means, electronic, mechanical, recording or otherwise, without the prior written permission of the authors and/or copyright holders.

The materials and information in this publication are provided as is, without representation, endorsement or warranty (express or implied) of any kind. This publication is designed to provide accurate and authoritative information about the subject matter covered, and best attempts have been made to provide the most accurate and valid information, but the publisher and authors do not warrant that the information is complete or free from inaccuracies. The publication is sold with the understanding that the publisher and authors are not engaged in rendering medical, psychological, financial, legal, or other professional services. If expert assistance or counseling is needed, the services of a competent professional should always be sought. For further legal information please refer to the Legal section at the back of this publication.

Warning: If you suffer from serious medical or psychological conditions, please consult your doctor or health-care professional before utilizing any of the patterns, exercises or information contained in this publication to ensure it is appropriate to do so.

Trademarks: All brand names and product names used in this book are trade names, service marks, trademarks, or registered trademarks of their respective owners. Neither the publisher nor the authors are associated with any product or vendor mentioned in this book. For permissions and specific trademark acknowledgements please refer to the Acknowledgements section at the back of this publication.

First Published 2014
TimeBinding Publications

Contents

	Introduction – Wisdom in action	9
1.	Autonomic Mode Patterns	27
2.	ANS Response Patterns	43
3.	Neural Syntax Patterns and Preferences	49
4.	Neural Integration Constraint (NIC) Patterns	55
5.	Communication Process Exploration	65
6.	Prime Functions Patterns and Preferences	79
7.	Core Competencies Patterns and Preferences	93
8.	Congruence and Alignment Patterns	105
9.	Highest Expressions Exploration	113
10.	Highest Expression Integration	141
11.	Trust Patterns Exploration	145
12.	Neural Integration Blocks (NIB's) Patterns	149
13.	Cognitive Dissonance Patterns	155
14.	*m*BIT Toolkit Category Patterns	161
15.	*mBraining* Discovery Exercises	181
16.	Wisdom, Emergence and Personal Evolution	187

Acknowledgements 199
Legal stuff 200
About the authors 201
References and resources 203

*m*BIT Coaching Workbook

Facilitators Guide

*m*BIT Coaching Workbook
Facilitators Guide

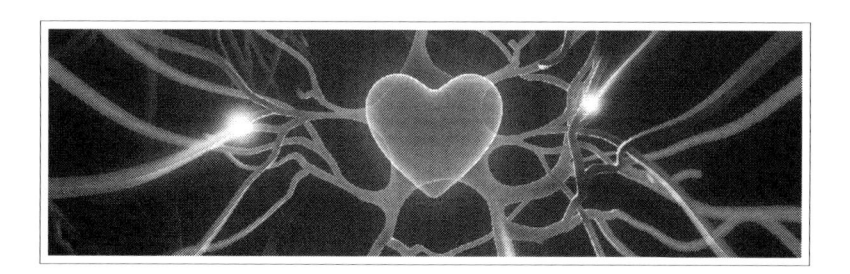

Introduction

"You have to master not only the art of listening to your head, you must also master listening to your heart and listening to your gut."

Carly Fiorina

As shown by numerous converging avenues of neuroscientific and behavioral modeling evidence, and described in detail in our book '*mBraining*', the *m*BIT model says that wisdom is generated through listening to and engaging the innate, intuitive intelligence of all your multiple brains (Heart, Head and Gut) via their Highest Expressions (Compassion, Creativity and Courage). The process for this is to:

1. Engage your neural networks or brains and communicate with them through conscious control of the autonomic gateways (for example by diaphragmatic breathing). Then enable them to communicate with each other.

2. Align your neural networks so you are congruent in your being and your responses.

3. Evolve your self/neural networks in order to function from higher levels of consciousness and the Highest Expressions of your authentic self.

4. Apply this higher level of consciousness and authentic self to practical life situations and thus have greater wisdom in your decisions and actions.

The key to this process is step 4 — in the application of multiple perspectives and Highest Expressions to pragmatic real-world situations. As the noted systems theorist, neuro-biologist and philosopher, Dr. Humberto Maturana highlights, *"All knowing is doing."* You only truly know something when you can use it with deep wisdom and insight to create real-world actions and results.

Wisdom in action

So as indicated, wisdom involves action and expression into the world. Wisdom that is not embodied in pragmatic action is not wisdom at all, it's merely entertaining ideas. Because wisdom only becomes true wisdom when it's pragmatically and consistently applied to practical life situations, this Workbook is designed to facilitate deep explorations into how you are *mBraining* your world — to how you are using your multiple brains in real world situations, in the patterns and behaviors you are using to create your world — and to highlight specific areas of application of the *mBIT* model, roadmap and principles to real world contexts. In conjunction with your *mBIT* Coach, this Workbook can truly assist you to deepen your wisdom and bring more integrated joy, happiness and success to evolve your world!

Facilitators Guide Introduction

*m*BIT Coach**ing** is a verb, a generative process and an ongoing journey into personal evolution. It's also a journey into increasing wisdom, happiness and success in life; into liberating the human spirit and bringing your Clients more alive. It is not meant to be, or designed to be, a one-shot deal. It's not a therapeutic intervention methodology. It's not aimed to '*fix broken people*' in a one-step session! Instead it's both action coaching and ontological coaching, that is, it's about generatively guiding and facilitating people into on-goingly evolving their world through a focus on both action and ways of being. As such, it's a process both of guiding people up the *m*BIT Roadmap to integrate their multiple brains through Highest Expression, and an ongoing exploration of how they are creating themselves, their worlds and the narrative of their lives.

This *m*BIT Coaching Workbook is a tool for working with Clients to open up a series of enquiries, to bring awareness to both the Client and the coach about the patterns and processes of how the Client is authoring their process of '*human becoming*'. As the neuro-biologist and systems philosopher, Humberto Maturana points out, "*we are not human beings, we are human becomings*", and *m*BIT Coaching embodies this understanding in both a deep and broad way. Our multiple brains are Darwinian selection systems that operate through ongoing neuro-genesis and neural plasticity to evolve neural networks that are optimal for the informational environments they are living in.

By deeply exploring the processes by which your Clients do *mBraining*, by which they connect both within themselves and across the many relationships that make up their life and world, you as an *m*BIT Coach are able to facilitate your Client to generatively learn and co-create an enriched informational environment that brings greater wisdom to their lives and ongoing evolution in choice, control, adaptability, resilience and novelty. With your Client, and using the foundational *m*BIT Coaching skills you've learned in your *m*BIT Coach Certification training, in conjunction with the tools, exercises and explorations in this *m*BIT Coaching Workbook, you can easily empower your Clients to increase the ecological complexity of their world. And since each person lives in a sphere of influence and entrainment, you thereby increase the wisdom and ecological complexity of your world too. Using the *m*BIT Coaching Workbook with your Clients becomes a win/win process.

So the *m*BIT Coaching Workbook is both a practical and pragmatic tool for enhancing your coaching practice as well as a mechanism for guiding the personal evolution journey. The Workbook brings a focus to your Clients on the components and processes of their *mBraining*. It adds value to their explorations between sessions. It gives you material to work through and uncovers directions for you to invest awareness, time and energy in during future coaching sessions. And it builds a database of insights for both yourself and each of your Clients. We trust and believe that you'll gain immense benefit and ongoing value from using the Workbook and its exercises both with yourself and your Clients and that it will add to your coaching practice in an evolutionary way.

*m*BIT Coaching as Generative Coaching

When Clients come to you, they typically want coaching around goals, issues, outcomes and challenges. They're usually focused on the '*content*' of their lives and want assistance and coaching in gaining success in this content – in the '*what*' of their lives. Whilst *m*BIT Coaching will certainly help people achieve content success since it helps get them aligned, motivated and congruent, this is not where the real power of *m*BIT Coaching arises.

You might therefore assume that *m*BIT Coaching is much more about coaching to process, especially since *m*BIT so strongly aligns with the NLP notion that '*process is more useful and important than content for facilitating change*'. And it's certainly true that *m*BIT Coaching focuses on the '*how*', on the processes that Clients use to create their reality, on how they are *mBraining* their lives. But the true power of advanced *m*BIT coaching lays far beyond this.

Where advanced *m*BIT Coaching really makes a transformational and evolutionary difference is by focusing on meta-process – focusing on the processes of process. This is where generative change begins to occur. This is where ongoing emergence and evolution of the Client's ontology (their way of being and doing) occurs. And facilitation of this process is the design outcome of this *m*BIT Coaching Workbook.

It's obvious isn't it, that when you are coaching for emergence, the level of wisdom and emergence that can arise is vitally dependent on the level of skill and self-awareness within the existing system. So the wisdom that can be generated is predicated on the Client's base skills. The more you can get a Client to become aware of their patterns and the patterns and processes of their patterns, the more you begin to educate and evolve their neural networks. By bringing awareness, self-reflection, conscious re-focus and choice about their unconscious processes, the ability to pattern-interrupt and the ability to perform new ways of doing their *mBraining*, the greater the skill base you and the Client generatively seed into their system and world. And this increases their capacity for greater wisdom and further emergence.

You see, you can definitely do useful *m*BIT Coaching by helping and guiding your Client up the *m*BIT Roadmap, and helping them explore wiser ways of being and doing around the issues, outcomes and challenges they present with. But you can truly take this to a whole 'nother level, through the ongoing journey of getting them to uncover the patterns and processes currently instantiated in their neural networks and lives and then doing *m*BIT Coaching on those processes. You start coaching the process of their processing and bringing greater wisdom and emergence to that meta-process level. And you continue to do this in deeper and higher ways, bringing more awareness to their multiple braining, feeding the patterns back into the patterning system as a way of highest expressing their *'being and doing'*. This is how you guide them as *'human becomings'*. And the exercises in the *m*BIT Coaching Workbook (along with the instructions in this Facilitators Guide) provide the tools and information you need on this generative journey up the *m*BIT Roadmap.

Utilizing the *m*BIT Coaching Workbook in your coaching practice, you truly open up even more opportunities to evolve their world, in the ongoing journey of *m*BIT Coach**ing**.

How to use this Workbook with your Client

There are two key ways you can use this *m*BIT Coaching Workbook with your Clients. First is to start at the beginning and work your way sequentially through the exercises, one part at a time, exploring your Client's patterns and processes and using the information and awareness gleaned via the Client's responses to the exercise questions as stimuli to guide your *m*BIT Coaching.

The other way is to trust your inner intuitive wisdom (via *m*BIT Roadmap facilitation of yourself) to find the most semantically dense, most generative exercises applicable for your Client at each point in the coaching journey. These can be the areas that your Client has the most challenges and weaknesses in and are therefore the points of greatest leverage and generative change. Alternatively, they may be the areas your Client has the most strengths in and can be used to build upon and support movement and change.

Whilst the exercises do tend to build upon one another as somewhat of a skill hierarchy, and are therefore synergistic and integrative, certain skills may already be well in play in your Client's *mBraining* and therefore not as beneficial as others for them. Either of the two ways of using the Workbook described above will be useful and add value to the Client and to the *m*BIT Coaching process. Trust your inner guidance on which of these is preferable with each individual Client and in each individual context as this may change across contexts and through time.

[**BTW:** Note that as a skills hierarchy, the list of exercise domains acts as a very useful diagnostic tool in its own right. You can examine each Client in the light of this list and use it to see where their strengths and weaknesses lay and how they may be missing particular skills that are required by other competencies dependent upon them.]

Workbook Outcomes

- The initial stimulus for this Workbook was to create an inexpensive and accessible tool to be used by *m*BIT Coaches to share with their Clients and help them work through and explore deeper issues and distinctions in the time between coaching sessions and thereby facilitate greater levels of generative learning and evolutionary change.

- In addition, this *'Coaches Facilitation Guide to Using the mBIT Coaching Workbook'* provides details about each section, how to use it, when and why to use it, what benefits it has, how to debrief it with the Client etc.

- There will also be *m*BIT Master Coach online trainings (and webinars) that teach Coaches how to use the Workbook both in coaching Clients and in marketing their services with Clients

Workbook Exercise Structure

The Workbook consists of 16 sections, each with a series of exercises.

Note: there are two contexts – general patterns in life and specific domains/issues.

The structure and outcomes for each exercise are:

- Education
- Self awareness / self calibration
- Self diagnosis
- Impact analysis
- Generative response elicitation
- Outcome setting for a coaching session

Notice that the flow moves from awareness, to skill gap analysis, and on through to positive and generative outcome elicitation. The underling approach with this is to get Clients exploring their inner and outer worlds, to uncover areas for growth and to leave them at the end of each exercise with a sense of hope, desire for change and a hunger to return to the next *m*BIT Coaching session, ready to bring forth emergent evolution in their ways of being and doing in their world.

As a Coach why you want to use the Workbook with Clients

There are a number of very important and pragmatic reasons why you'd want to utilize the *m*BIT Coaching Workbook with Clients to augment and enhance their *m*BIT coaching experience:

- **Perception Management** - The Workbook provides a glossy, professional, high quality tactile/visual symbol of the *m*BIT/Neuroscience based coaching process they have been experiencing. It provides a tangible object that the Client takes away from the Coaching session to their work or home and creates a positive and powerful anchor to remind and evoke the Coaching success state in their personal home/work context. Having a glossy and *'cool'* looking Workbook is far more attractive and builds much stronger perception management than just printed or photocopied pages or a binder.

- **Deeper Integration and Exploration** – By using the Workbook and exploring exercises between Coaching sessions, the Client and Coach are able to uncover powerful information to deepen the integration and to explore in subsequent Coaching sessions. Getting Clients to work on '*homeplay*' exercises between sessions increases the value and salience of the Coaching sessions and ensures a greater likelihood of transfer and integration into the home and work contexts, while also increasing the likelihood of the Client maintaining an active and ongoing Coaching relationship.

- **Ongoing Identity Anchor** – As the Client works through more and more sections of the Workbook and writes, explores and integrates their thoughts and feelings onto the pages of the Workbook, it creates a strong anchor to their deep core values and identity. In this way the Workbook (and therefore the Coaching work and relationship) become more strongly identified with, valued and appreciated. The more the Workbook is used, the more the Client '*owns*' it, the stronger the ongoing anchor becomes to remind the Client of the importance and value of returning for more Coaching. Every time they see the Workbook and its glossy '*cool*' cover in their work or home they will be positively reminded about the success of their *m*BIT Coaching work and their personal evolution. By having their writing, their thoughts and feelings recorded in a glossy perfect-bound book, it's like they are creating the ongoing story of their personal evolution, their own '*book of their life*', and this will be far stronger as a metaphor and anchor than just a bunch of pages in a binder or photocopied pages. The book metaphor is a powerful subconscious influence.

- **Effort Increases Value** – Research in the field of Behavioral Economics has shown that, as the amount of effort people put into an experience increases, the perceived value it has increases correspondingly by a large amount (e.g. see Norton, Mochon & Ariely, 2011). This is known as the '*Ikea Effect*', since it has been found that furniture people have to build themselves becomes far more valued and appreciated compared with the same price furniture they have put no effort into. By having Clients work through exercises and put effort into the exploration and integration processes, they'll come to unconsciously value the experience and your Coaching services more. The Workbook acts as a physical and emotional mechanism to focus them on doing the additional work and effort, and they can clearly see the amount of effort they've completed as the Workbook gets filled with their writing and achievements with doing the exercises. And the more they value the *m*BIT processes, the more their heart engages in the process, and the stronger they'll be in appreciating and using their new insights and skills.

[Reference: Norton, M. I., Mochon, D. & Ariely, D. *The IKEA Effect: When Labor Leads to Love*, Harvard Business School Marketing Unit Working Paper, (11-091), 2011.]

- **Own Idea Bias** – Research in Behavioral Economics has also shown that people have a strong bias towards their own ideas (e.g. see Ariely, 2010). This is an extension of the Ikea Effect but applied to the creation of ideas. Once someone has written down or expressed an idea, they *'own'* it, and it becomes much more valuable and they'll expend more time and effort on it and on taking action on it. So by getting Clients to do the exploration and journaling exercises in the Workbook, they will express their own thinking and ideas and therefore value and live them more strongly compared to just hearing about them from the Coach.

[Reference: Ariely, D. *The Upside of Irrationality*, Harper, 2010.]

*m*BIT Coaching Workbook Exercises

The *m*BIT Coaching Workbook contains the following exercise sections for your Client to explore:

1. Autonomic Mode Patterns – Sympathetic vs Parasympathetic Mode
2. ANS Response Patterns – Fight versus Flight versus Freeze versus Fold versus Tend and Befriend Patterns
3. Neural Syntax Patterns and Preferences
4. Neural Integration Constraint (NIC) Patterns and Preferences
5. Communication Process Exploration
6. Prime Functions Patterns and Preferences
7. Core Competencies Patterns and Preferences
8. Congruence and Alignment Patterns
9. Highest Expressions Exploration
10. Highest Expression Integration
11. Trust Patterns Exploration
12. Neural Integration Blocks (NIB's) Patterns and Preferences
13. Cognitive Dissonance Patterns
14. *m*BIT Toolkit Category Patterns
15. *mBraining* Discovery Exercises
16. Wisdom, Emergence and Personal Evolution

Facilitators Guide

Note that this list of exercise domains can be viewed loosely as a skills-hierarchy of competencies needed to live from generative wisdom, Highest Expression and aligned *mBraining*. For example, it's fairly obvious that if a person has limiting patterns in, or lacks skill in, controlling their autonomic mode they'll be challenged in the higher components of the *m*BIT Roadmap. Similarly, it's going to be difficult to access and align the Highest Expressions if there are issues with Neural Integration Constraints or problems with communication processes between the multiple brains. In order to do behavioral excellence in generative wisdom, you need the underlying base skills at sufficient levels of competence.

Viewed in this way, the list acts as a very useful diagnostic tool in its own right. You can examine and explore with each Client their skills, strengths and opportunities for growth in the light of this list and use it to determine which of their strengths to best use. You can also use the list to discover if your Client is missing any particular skills that are required by other competencies dependent upon those skills.

Coaching to Emergence vs Compliance

Coaching for compliance is when a Coach tries to "fix" the Client, or help the Client to "fix" themselves. Such an approach is in some ways more like therapy and often involves telling the Client what they must or should do. Research by neuroscientist and coaching expert, Prof. Richard Boyatzis and his colleagues, over many years and many studies (e.g. Boyatzis, Smith & Van Oosten, 2010; Boyatzis, Smith & Blaize, 2006) has shown that this compliance approach often tips people into stress, sympathetic arousal, and what Boyatzis calls the '*NEA*' (Negative Emotional Attractor). It can also engender a sense of obligation and leave the Client dependent, limited and ultimately stuck. Certainly, stress and sympathetic arousal down-regulates cognitive ability, resilience and even decreases peripheral vision and awareness. People literally become myopic, uncreative and less able to find resourceful solutions when stuck in the stressed or NEA state.

Boyatzis and colleagues, on the other hand, have found that *'coaching with compassion'*, triggers what is called the *'PEA'* (Positive Emotional Attractor) and leads to increases in parasympathetic balance. This in turn switches on areas of the brain associated with creativity, connection and possibility. So coaching to Highest Expression and coaching to emergence are what *m*BIT Coaching and this Workbook are all about. It's never about trying to "fix" a Client or their issues. Instead, it's about bringing a resonant sense of Compassion, Creativity and Courage to both the Client and the coaching relationship/experience in order to evoke curiosity, creativity and a climate of positive emotional exploration.

Therefore you can truly enjoy working with your Client on the exercise domains above, using them as guides to focus the Client on possibility, on areas of exploration, and on domains to bring themselves, their relationships and their world more alive!

Strengths vs Weaknesses

In the field of Positive Psychology over the last decade or so there's been a growing body of research showing that when people focus on their strengths it helps increase levels of happiness, resilience and positivity. This is well and good and as an *m*BIT Coach, you want to use this approach with your Client as much as possible.

However, strengths overused can become weaknesses. What you're best at is often what you're most likely to take too far. There is a *'bliss-point'* for the use of strengths, an optimal amount. Any strength overused can become a liability or weakness. This is what the great sage Ralph Waldo Emerson meant when he warned: "Stand in terror of your talents."

"Any virtue carried to an extreme can become a crime."

Alexandre Dumas

"What may appear to be the source of one's strength can often also be the source of one's weakness."

Chin-Ning Chu

"We've seen virtually every strength taken too far: confidence to the point of hubris, and humility to the point of diminishing oneself. We've seen vision drift into aimless dreaming, and focus narrow down to tunnel vision. Show us a strength and we'll give you an example where its overuse has compromised performance and probably even derailed a career."

Robert B. Kaiser and Robert E. Kaplan

Research by Robert Kaiser and colleagues (e.g. Kaiser & Kaplan, 2013 ; Kaiser & Overfield, 2011) has shown that while strengths-based development has become a popular approach in management and leadership, a focus on maximizing natural talents rather than trying to correct weaknesses has ironically lead managers to turn their strengths into weaknesses through overuse. It has also caused them to neglect shortcomings that degrade the performance of employees, teams, and organizations.

So focusing too much on strengths alone can be counterproductive in a Client's life. Yes, we want to facilitate Clients to use their strengths, but not at the overall cost of their success and personal evolution.

Weaknesses as Skill-gaps and Opportunities

It's also vitally important as a Coach to help your Client explore, focus on and strengthen their skill-gaps, since a chain is only as strong as its weakest link.

> *"You cannot run away from a weakness; you must sometimes fight it out or perish. And if that be so, why not now, and where you stand?"*
>
> Robert Louis Stevenson

As an *m*BIT Coach utilizing this Workbook, both you and your Clients need ongoing awareness that strengthening areas of weakness is NOT about fixing broken problems. Instead it's about expressing the courage to creatively explore areas of opportunity. Our weaknesses represent negative '*strange attractors*' in the complex non-linear dynamics of our human lives. We tend to end up spiraling into these attractors during times of stress, overwhelm or when we aren't paying attention. So by facilitating your Clients in building up their skill-gaps, by strengthening their areas of decreased competency and skill, they learn to increase their overall resilience, and ensure their systems are set to truly flourish.

Especially note that in working on building skills and competencies in areas where the Client does not yet have natural aptitudes or existing strengths, is definitely NOT about '*shoulds*'. It's not about modal operators of necessity. It's about possibility and choice. It's about having the freedom to transcend ways of limiting themselves. So flexibly ensure your Client understands this orientation. And listen for any modal operators they are using in their language when they talk about working on areas uncovered by the Workbook exercises. If you hear them saying, "I must fix this", "I should work on that", then please interrupt those linguistic and thinking patterns and guide them in expressing their model of world in a more generative way. Encourage them to use modal operators of possibility and desire. Get them to talk about what they'd like to do, what would be possible for them to do, to explore and talk about their vision for change and increasing skill development. Don't let them *'should all over themselves'*.

Encourage your Clients to explore the gaps in relation to their ideal sense of self, their Highest Expression of self'ing, to see (and feel, and hear) themselves transcending the skill-gaps, getting stronger, more competent, more flexible, more resilient. Guide them to create compelling visions around building their skills in the areas uncovered, so that working on this becomes a Positive Emotional Attractor, and not a negatively perceived or stressful experience.

Another benefit of not just focusing on strengths, but instead utilizing less-used competencies, is that this opens up novelty into the Client's system and encourages new neural pathways to form in their multiple brains, allowing for the stimulus of neural plasticity. Indeed, new work in the field of network complexity theory is showing that one way to make things better and improve overall network function is to remove or block the most optimal components from the system (for example see Mullins, 2014). This is known as *'Braess's Paradox'*, and has been found to function in complex network systems as diverse as the human brain, transport networks, metabolic diseases and ecological niches. So not focusing on strengths, but instead putting attention on lesser-used skills, can allow a system to begin to function in optimally new ways.

Bringing a sense of playfulness and curiosity to this experience will also be very useful for evoking their natural creativity with this, and help stimulate their neural-plasticity as they continue to evolve their world with the help of the Workbook exercises and your wonderful, generative and supportive *m*BIT coaching.

References:

Boyatzis, R.E., Smith, M. & Blaize, N., *Developing sustainable leaders through coaching and compassion*, Academy of Management Journal on Learning and Education, 5(1): 8-24, 2006.

Boyatzis, R.E., Smith, M. & Van Oosten, E., *Coaching for Change*, People Matters, pp. 68 – 71, June 2010.

Kaiser, Robert B. & Kaplan, Robert E., *Learn to Fear Your Strengths to Become a Better Leader*, Training Magazine, April 3, 2013.

Kaiser, Robert B. & Overfield, Darren V., *Strengths, strengths overused, and lopsided leadership*, Consulting Psychology Journal: Practice and Research, Vol 63(2), 89-109, June 2011.

Mullins, J., Less is more: To make things better, try making them worse, NewScientist, Vol 221, No. 2952, p. 30 – 33, 18 Jan 2014.

How to do the exercises

1. Get your Client to do the exercises when they are not rushed, when they have time, space and a conducive environment to explore the questions and deeply involve themselves in the enquiries. Guide them to not just do the exercises from their *'head'*, but also involve their heart and gut. Suggest they meditate on them, chew over them, dwell on them in their heart. Explore them deeply.

2. Guide your Client to do the exercises firstly in their *'normal'* state and then redo them from an aligned and balanced state. Remind them to take a couple of minutes to do Balanced Breathing using the Highest Expressions and the *m*BIT Foundational Sequence. (Ensure that you teach and guide them through this experience.) Instruct your Client to then do the questions again and note what changes. Do they get different or additional insights and distinctions when in a balanced mode?

3. Ensure your Client understands that there are no wrong or right answers with these exercises. They're designed to be journeys of exploration into how they are *'mBraining'* their life – how they are using their multiple brains to create their world and reality. Each of us has patterns and habits – unconscious competencies – that our neural networks, as patterning systems, perform for us. In order to evolve their world, your Clients need to first become aware of their existing patterns, then they need to explore these patterns, the outcomes they create and the underlying values and secondary gains that support them, and then they need to align and integrate around them, to evolve their intentions, actions and consequences and ultimately their brains and the very neural networks that bring forth their identity and their world.

4. Remind them that after they have finished an Exercise, they should take a moment to fill in the *'Generative Learning: Future Pacing the next mBIT Coaching Session'* section at the end of the exercise. This is designed to help them generalize their learnings, open up their unconscious and conscious minds to new possibilities, encourage them to ask themselves *'what else?, where else?, what if?'*, and to future pace their insights and learnings into the next coaching session and thereby make the most of their work and time with you.

5. Most importantly, encourage them to have fun with exploring these exercises. Guide them to bring a sense of creativity and playfulness to how they approach this. The design of the exercises is to first bring awareness to their inner and outer worlds and their patterns and unconscious competencies. Next they help the Client uncover skill gaps and opportunities for growth and personal evolution. Finally, they engender experiences of possibility, hope and a sense of a higher expression of self, that working together with you, the Client can more deeply explore and bring to life at their next *m*BIT Coaching session. And of course, with their innate intuitive intelligence at play, they can be delightfully surprised at what emerges and evolves in their world.

Generative Learning: Future Pacing the next *m*BIT Coaching Session

At the end of each exercise section you will find there's a *'Generative Learning: Future Pacing the next mBIT Coaching Session'* page. The idea and outcome of this page is to assist and encourage the Client to go *'meta'* to their own *mBraining* processes, to be self-reflective and to explore the learnings inherent in the exercises. This installs a process of generative learning and is what you as an *m*BIT Coach are aiming to setup and facilitate. To do this, discuss with your Client how you want them to reflect. Engage them in an enquiry on learning about how they learn to learn, how they learn from their experience and generalize this into their life and how they notice patterns of learning and response to their lives.

It's about exploring how they experience their learnings and process them at a head, heart and gut level. Do they get upset when they find something they don't like about their habits and patterns and where do they feel or process that? Do they get curious? Do they stay calm and balanced? Do they get determined and motivated to learn and explore? Do they bring self-compassion to their explorations and learning processes? Remember that in facilitating change in the human system, *'the heart leads'*, so the more your Client can value and appreciate the learning and exploration process, and the more they can bring curiosity and creativity to the experience, the greater the generative wisdom that can emerge in the learning process.

The page contains sections for:

Reflections and Learnings

Points to discuss at the next session

Coaching outcomes I'd like to pursue/explore

So this page is also about *'future pacing'* i.e. setting up future outcomes and behavioral intentions and actions. This also assists in the process of generalization of their learnings and gives you and the Client insights and actions to work with in the subsequent *m*BIT Coaching session.

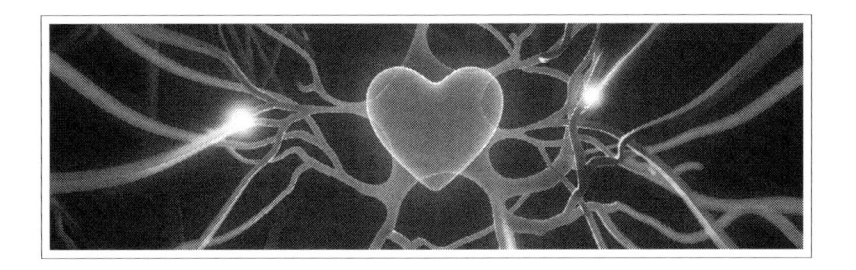

1.

Autonomic Mode

In order to work effectively and gain skills with your multiple brains and their functions and competencies, it helps to understand the role of your Autonomic Nervous System (ANS) and how it affects the quality of the way your brains operate.

Your nervous system has two major divisions, the voluntary and the autonomic. The Voluntary System is mainly concerned with movement and sensation. The Autonomic Nervous System on the other hand is responsible for control of involuntary and visceral bodily functions. The functions it controls include:

- Cardiovascular
- Respiratory
- Digestive
- Urinary
- Reproductive functions
- The body's response to stress

It's called *'autonomic'* because it operates largely automatically and outside of conscious control. It's divided into two separate branches — the sympathetic and parasympathetic. These two branches work in a delicately tuned, reciprocal and (usually) opposing fashion. Simplistically, the sympathetic system can be considered to be the *'fight or flight'* system. It allows the body to function under stress and danger. The parasympathetic system is the *'feeding and fornicating'* arm. It controls the vegetative functions of feeding, breeding, rest and repose. The parasympathetic system also provides constant opposition to the sympathetic system to bring your total system into balance or homeostasis.

In times of danger or stress, the sympathetic system, which has a very fast onset and response, kicks in and gets you moving to handle or resolve the situation. The slower acting parasympathetic system begins to operate after the danger has passed, and brings you back to normalcy. Without the opposing function of the parasympathetic system your body would stay amped up, burning energy and fuel and eventually exhaust itself.

Why is this important?

The reason you want to know about the sympathetic and parasympathetic systems is because they innervate and impact the heart, gut and head brains. There are major connections between the head brain hemispheres, the cardiac brain, the enteric brain and these sympathetic and parasympathetic arms of the ANS. And as the two ANS components work in opposing ways, the dominance of one or the other leads to very different modes of processing throughout our multiple brains. In this way the *'Autonomic Mode'* strongly influences how the multiple brains operate.

For example, in the gut, parasympathetic activity enhances intestinal peristaltic movement promoting nourishment during quiescence, whereas sympathetic activity inhibits such activity during times when physical exertion requires catabolic (energy) mobilization. Parasympathetic activity generally slows the heart, whereas sympathetic activity accelerates it.

You'll notice here that a powerful functional principle of opponent processing is operating for autonomic control across your total system. Your brains can function in ways that are sympathetic dominant, parasympathetic dominant, or some combination of the two, and each of these systems typically opposes the other. You can see this opponent processing clearly at work by examining details of what each system activates.

Sympathetic activation

Activation of the sympathetic nervous system has the following effects:

- Dilates the pupils and opens the eyelids
- Stimulates the sweat glands
- Dilates the blood vessels in the large skeletal muscles
- Constricts the blood vessels in the rest of the body
- Increases heart rate
- Relaxes and opens up the bronchial tubes of the lungs
- Contracts the sphincter of the bladder and the bladder wall relaxes
- Shuts down and inhibits the secretions in the digestive system
- Can lead to involuntary defecation
- Is associated with Right Hemisphere activation and dominance in the head brain

Parasympathetic activation

Activation of the parasympathetic nervous system has the following effects:

- Constricts the pupils
- Activates and increases the secretion of the salivary glands
- Stimulates the secretions of the stomach
- Decreases heart rate
- Constricts the bronchial tubes and stimulates secretions in the lungs
- Stimulates the activity of the gastro intestinal tract
- Is involved in sexual arousal
- Is associated with Left Hemisphere activation and dominance in the head brain

In this section of the Workbook, you will explore your patterns of Autonomic mode and sympathetic or parasympathetic response and dominance. We each have differing patterns, habits and preferences for orienting to stress and to the world. Some people have tendencies to always operate from a sympathetic or stress dominance. Others tend to be down-regulated and operating largely from states of parasympathetic dominance. Or you might flip between these in various ways and amounts. Each of us is different, and can respond differently in a variety of contexts and situations. Knowing about your typical patterns and preferences, your *'unconscious competencies'* can increase your self-awareness and allow you to begin gaining more choice, control and wisdom in how you are driving and using your multiple brains.

Facilitators Guide

This section on Autonomic mode is designed to explore your Client's patterns and habits of ANS mode skills and the way autonomic mode typically plays out in their life and in specific contexts. You are looking for overall patterns and triggers as well as strengths, weaknesses, blockages and limitations. This will show what their base levels of state control are and their unconscious ways of using their brains (sympathetic, parasympathetic, balanced or meta-stable). The main focus on coaching of this is to bring more awareness and competency to their control of Autonomic Mode. And of course, this involves them being able to notice their mode and then use the appropriate breathing pattern and guided visualization and kinesthetic experience to evoke the required mode.

State Dependency

As you remember from *m*BIT Coach Certification training, neural networks exhibit state dependent activation. This shows up in classic psychological processes such as *'mood dependent memory'* and *'state dependent learning'*, etc. as well as in NLP with the notion that *'states carry strategies'*. A great and entertaining example of state dependent memory and learning comes from John Elliotson's book, "Human Physiology".

> *"Dr. Abel informed me of an Irish porter to a warehouse, who forgot, when sober, what he had done when drunk: but, being drunk, again recollected the transactions of his former state of intoxication. On one occasion, being drunk, he had lost a parcel of some value, and in his sober moments could give no account of it. Next time he was intoxicated, he recollected that he had left the parcel at a certain house, and there being no address on it, it had remained there safely, and was got on his calling for it. This man must have had two souls, one for his sober state, and one for him when drunk."*
>
> [Reference: Elliotson, John, *Human Physiology*, Longman Press, London, 1835.]

State dependent activation is a powerful and over-riding neural effect, so it's vital that your Client learns to control their ANS state or mode. However, it's important to note that if someone has spent their life in a state of ANS sympathetic arousal for example, then they'll have installed the majority of their state dependent learnings and unconscious competencies in this state or mode. So their reference structures for all sorts of skills and strategies will be filtered through and dependent on that ANS state. This means you'll have to help them generalize their life skills and competencies into the more functional and adaptive ANS Balanced Mode.

It's like someone who has spent their life chronically bent over. Such a posture is not a physiologically functional and optimal way to live, bent and hunched over. However, when you first get them to straighten up, the muscles that have spent years cramped or overly stretched will now have to straighten out and at first this will hurt. The person will not feel like the newly straightened and balanced posture is comfortable. The old pattern will feel far more comfortable and familiar, even though it causes all sorts of systemic long term stress and damage. The new straight, *'aligned in gravity'* posture will be healthier and take less overall energy to maintain. But to the person who has been chronically bent, the straight posture will take time to become comfortable with and skilled in. Learning to use new ANS modes will be experienced similarly. You'll need to coach your Client into the more adaptive ways of using their ANS and accessing the competencies that belong with a balanced ANS.

Exploring Your Autonomic Mode Patterns

This section explores the patterns of Autonomic mode your Client does habitually. This provides you and the Client with insights into their default preferences and habits in how they respond to stressors in their world. And gives you areas to increase their awareness, skills and competencies in.

> *Do you have any overall patterns of Autonomic Nervous System (ANS) mode in your life? For example, are you chronically stressed, hyper-vigilant or in high energy mode (sympathetic dominant mode)? Or are you typically tired, depressed, suffer from malaise or in low energy, recuperation mode (parasympathetic dominant mode)? Or do you flip between these states?*

Here you'll find out if there are patterns and propensities for ANS mode in your Client's life. Are they chronically sympathetic dominant, hypervigilant etc.? Or are they chronically depressed and parasympathetic dominant etc.? A person's patterns of using their ANS are incredibly important since it strongly influences which competencies the multiple brains can easily evoke and operate from. For example, when depressed, a person is unlikely to want to or be able to dream, plan or focus on holding outcomes as important values, since their heart will be down-regulated into parasympathetic over-dominant competencies. Similarly, the head brain will not be able to think clearly and will be likely to succumb to distorted and pessimistic cognitive perceptions and meaning. Equally, the gut brain will not be in a state to access courage, motility and a strong, robust and vital sense of core-self'ing.

Understanding the causes and secondary-gains (hidden benefits) of the Client's patterns is also important here. And more important still, is showing the Client how to pattern-interrupt the old habits and move to more adaptive and generative states. You'll need to teach them Balanced Breathing and really work with them to use their neuro-physiology and Neural Integrative Engagements (NIE's) to strongly shift to a balanced ANS mode at will. Practice will be the key here; they'll need to do daily practice so that they build the neural patterns and propensity for accessing Balanced Mode. And if you know how to do NLP Anchoring, then you can help them by providing a strong resource anchor for the ANS Balanced mode.

❓ *Are there triggers, contexts, people or situations that put you into sympathetic dominant (stressed) mode?*

This is important as it indicates control leverage points i.e. contextual points that the Client can use to facilitate more adaptive responding. So you'll want to coach your Client to emerge a more adaptive, generative and wiser response to the triggers, giving them choice. Run the Client through the *m*BIT Highest Expression Foundational Sequence around the trigger situation(s) and explore what outcomes and meaning each brain makes of this, and then align the brains around an outcome of a more generative response. And make sure you future pace (do a mental rehearsal and walk through of a likely upcoming instance of the trigger situation) to test and ensure the new response is associated to the old trigger context.

What's also important here is the notion of *'Cause and Effect'* thinking. As an *m*BIT Coach, you want to bring your Client to a sense of choice, control, flexibility and efficacy. A lot of people typically think that external situations and events *'cause'* their emotional responses. In that way they give up control to the external environment and to other people. Instead, you'll want to coach your Client into taking back the locus of control. They are at choice in how they respond to the exigencies of the world. So ensure your Client knows that the situation doesn't *'cause'* the response, they make their own meaning and can choose to respond generatively rather than merely react – it's really about how the Client is consciously (and unconsciously) choosing to respond – it's their own *'response-ability'*.

And remember to make sure you are watching for the Client's breathing patterns with this coaching exercise, and that they are able to adeptly bring balanced breathing to the situation to calm the sympathetic dominant responding.

? *Are there triggers, contexts, people or situations that put you into parasympathetic dominant (low energy, depressed) mode?*

Refer to the point above, but apply it for parasympathetic dominance versus sympathetic dominance. Note that parasympathetic mode can often be a rebound effect whereby the ANS and the multiple brains attempt to bring the person back to homeostasis after the occurrence of a stressor (and that sometimes this stressor may be outside of the person's conscious awareness, and they only consciously notice the overarching depressed state).

In some cases you may need to bring the Client to a slightly higher energy mode to lift them out of the low energy state before taking them to Balanced Mode. This is known as Autonomic Counterbalancing. This would be the case where they are so low in energy and depressed that you need them to come alive enough to even begin to really engage in the coaching process. However, be wary of retriggering a stress response and thereby provoking a bi-stable bounce between sympathetic and parasympathetic modes.

A case study example may be of use and interest here. We had a Client come to us for *m*BIT Coaching who presented with a depressed and parasympathetic dominant mode that had recently occurred, but from which they were unable to lift themselves out of. Our first step was to check if the person had a history of depression and whether they needed psychological or medical intervention before any *m*BIT Coaching could occur on this issue. With no previous history of depression, we then explored whether there was a precipitating event that lead to the current state. It turned out that the Client's wife had recently been overseas for an extended period in a third-world country and while there, a major environmental catastrophe had occurred and the Client had not been able to contact her for nearly 3 weeks, during which time he feared she had been hurt or killed. This had caused him an extended period of chronic and intense sympathetic dominant stress mode.

Eventually his wife was able to contact him to say she was alright and was able to fly back home. However, from the point of stress relief onwards he had experienced a debilitating parasympathetic dominant mode and lost all motivation, energy and will, and from this mode was unable to lift himself back up. This was obviously a parasympathetic rebound effect from the extended sympathetic state. His overly parasympathetic state made it challenging for him to even begin doing balanced breathing and lift his predominant state back to normalcy, so to start we tasked him to do a weekend of hiking with a group of his friends. The gentle and aerobic sympathetic elevation of hiking and exercise for the extended period of a whole weekend was all he needed to bring his energy levels up and balance his ANS, and from that state we were then able to *m*BIT coach him into generative and optimal emergence.

You will also need to do *m*BIT Coaching on any head-based narratives they may be running that are causing the depressing of their mind/body system, should this be the triggering process. If this is the case, there are three factors you may consider working with to help your Client. The first is the content of their internal dialogue. You can help your Client become aware of any limiting language patterns that may be triggering their depressed state.

The second is the quality of how their internal dialogue sounds. For example, if they are speaking to themselves in a slow, low tone, monotonous manner, have them speed up their internal dialogue, make it higher pitched and with a wide range of vocal variety. This will instantly begin to shift their overall internal state.

Third, you will want to help your Client dissociate from their internal narrative. Help them to observe their own internal dialogue and to be separate from it. Once they can become subjectively distanced, get them to experience it as *'just a story they were running in their head'* and not something that has objective meaning or *'truth'*. Facilitate them to begin to feel balanced and comfortable as they watch themselves create the less than functional narrative.

Humans are inherently creative. They cannot not create. However, they can become aware that they are the designers and creators of their stories, they are always at choice once they know how to step back from the story, dissociate from the state they were unconsciously creating, and choose a more creative and generative response. And your job as a Coach is to facilitate this process with your Clients.

Note also that a chronic depressed and parasympathetic dominant state can be triggered by various health issues. People with damage to their hearts and blocked arteries often report malaise and depression. One Client related to us how he had experienced a period of unexplained low energy and mild emotional/psychological depression that had no obvious cause for approximately 6 months before succumbing finally to cardiac infarct and needing bypass surgery. His heart brain had obviously been trying to inform him of the pending problem and had down-regulated his ANS mode in order to minimize stress to his overloaded heart muscles.

Parasympathetic dominance can also be caused by impacts on immune function due to viral infections, toxic metal poisoning and other environmental triggers. So look for the causes and triggers of unexplained chronic states and refer your Client to an appropriate health professional if there is any evidence the underlying causes are organic or medical. It is always better to err on the side of caution and have your Client get a full medical health check.

What strategies do you typically use to shift yourself from overly sympathetic dominant (stressed) mode?

Here you will learn about how the Client balances their ANS mode through learned strategies and behaviors. Typical ways in which people bring themselves back to homeostasis are to use parasympathetic activities such as food, sexuality, relaxation and meditation. Your Client's strategies may be functional and useful or they may be the cause of negative systemic issues in their life. You are looking for both how wise and ecological their strategies are as well as how much self-awareness the Client has around these strategies. Ultimately, you want to educate the Client into having a wider range of wise choices and control in how they notice and shift ANS mode.

You may also find it useful to teach the Client the *m*BIT *'StopStress'* breathing technique (which works using the principle of Autonomic Counterbalancing described in *mBraining*):

"If you find yourself getting stressed, angry, frightened or any other form of Sympathetic ANS response: Stop, take a breath for 2 seconds in, and 10 seconds out. Repeat 5 times. This will quickly calm you down. Then begin to breathe for 6 (approx.) seconds in, 6 seconds out. This is called Balanced Breathing, and requires the inbreath and outbreath to be of the same duration, and will bring the ANS into balance i.e. a balance between sympathetic and parasympathetic. It is calming and healthful. Add into the breathing process that you imagine with every breath your heart, mind and body is filling with a beautiful peaceful loving joy. Breathe this into your heart, up to your head and then down to your gut."

Other strategies you can encourage your Client to use, to decrease their sympathetic responding and conversely increase their parasympathetic mode, and thereby bring more balance include:

- Relaxation of the gateways (eyes, tongue, throat, diaphragm, hands, feet, pelvis etc.)
- Cold-water face immersion – bathing the face with cold water
- Eating and drinking (appropriately and healthfully)
- Intimacy and Loving Sexuality
- HRV Biofeedback
- Mindfulness of the body (proprioceptive focus)
- Warm relaxing bath (supine position increases parasympathetic dominance)
- Meditation
- Gentle walk (especially in nature)

- Yawning
- Stroking the upper lip
- Breathing parasympathetic activating fragrances (aromatherapy e.g. using Lavender or Bergamot, both of which have been shown in research to increase parasympathetic modulation)
- Focus on the Positive: practicing loving-kindness, compassion, tranquility, peace, joy and other positive balancing emotions
- Relaxing music
- Negative Ions – breathing negative air ions has been shown to decrease sympathetic mode and increase parasympathetic modulation
- Grounding – connecting your bare feet to the ground/earth increases parasympathetic activation

What strategies do you typically use to shift yourself from overly parasympathetic dominant (depressed) mode?

Here you will learn about how the Client balances their ANS mode when it is overly parasympathetic. Typical ways in which people bring themselves back to homeostasis are to use sympathetic activities such as exercise, adrenalin inducing sports and activities, games, watching action movies and anything that increases energy levels and gets the heart racing. As in the previous item, your Client's strategies may be functional and useful or they may be the cause of negative systemic issues in their life. You are looking for both how wise and ecological their strategies are as well as how much self-awareness they have around their strategies. Ultimately, you want to educate the Client into having a wider range of wise choices and control in how they shift ANS mode.

You may also find it useful to teach the Client the *m*BIT '*StopDepress*' breathing technique (which works using the principle of Autonomic Counterbalancing described in *mBraining*):

"If you find yourself getting depressed, emotionally down or any other form of Parasympathetic ANS response: Stop, take a breath for 10 seconds in, and 2 seconds out. Repeat 5 times. This will pump you up, fill you with energy. Then begin to breathe for 6 (approx.) seconds in, 6 seconds out. This is called Balanced Breathing, and requires the inbreath and outbreath to be of the same duration, and will bring the ANS into balance i.e. a balance between sympathetic and parasympathetic. It is enlivening and healthful. Add into the breathing process that you imagine with every breath your heart, mind and body is filling with a beautiful sparkling and loving joy. Breathe this into your heart, up to your head and then down to your gut."

Are you able to notice or calibrate what mode you are in during your day? Do you have good awareness levels about your state and whether you are overly stressed or depressed? Are you easily able to track your stress and energy levels? What strategies do you use to track your state and to notice 'how' you are creating your own responses and 'reality'?

This is truly about awareness and meta-awareness. Wisdom requires awareness and the ability to make refined distinctions. Experts have more distinctions than novices. So in debriefing this with your Client, bring their attention to how they '*do*' their noticing and tracking of their own internal processes and how they track for what their ANS is doing across and within the contexts and situations of their life. Are there some contexts in which they do excellent self-awarenessing? Are there other contexts in which they lose the ability to stay aware and meta to their processes? What is the difference and how can they learn to gain more self-awareness, and ultimately thereby choice?

Note of course that in some contexts it is not appropriate to split attention and that being in flow, fully associated and with no meta-awareness is what is required for competent performance. However, having strategies to unconsciously track for ANS mode and to go meta and notice after the performance has completed, what mode was operating and what can be learned to improve the performance, is an important way we increase skill, expertise and wisdom. This of course is one of the useful functions of this Workbook for the Client. It helps them begin to reflect on their processes and make distinctions that they might not otherwise do. The act of answering the questions in this Workbook, builds neural circuits for reflecting on their actions, processes and strategies.

> *Are you able to notice and calibrate what your breathing is doing during your day? Do you have good awareness of your breathing patterns, both the timing and duration of your in-breaths and out-breaths, as well as which part of your lungs you are breathing from (high in the chest, middle of the chest, diaphragm etc.)? How can you bring even more attention to this? What impacts will this have on your life?*

Refer to the point above, but apply it for breathing patterns. Breathing is a key gateway for control of ANS mode and for state shift. So you want your Client both to truly appreciate how important awareness and control of breathing is, as well as what impacts this will have across their life. What would improve? How will control of breathing change their health, mood, relationships, energy levels, etc.? The debrief of this question allows you to put focus on coaching them in deep diaphragmatic Balanced Breathing and various other breathing techniques, to give them greater distinctions and skills in the simple yet powerful art of breathing. You can also set them up and future pace them doing this in various contexts and specific situations. Focus them on both a sense of *'Balanced Breathing in Action'* and the calibration and tracking of *'Breathing through Action'* – noticing in context how they are breathing and controlling their ANS mode.

What are the activities, things, people or experiences that make you feel revitalized, calm, refreshed and renewed? How can you plan for and make time for more of these in your life? What will a more balanced, renewed and vital you feel like? What difference will this make in your life?

When a person spends too long in either overly sympathetic or overly parasympathetic modes, their energy levels are depleted and they lose their vitality and zest. This question explores what brings your Client alive – what revitalizes their spirit. Help them make distinctions on this and bring to conscious awareness both how they can rebalance and re-energize themselves, as well as the importance of fitting these activities into their normal life schedule.

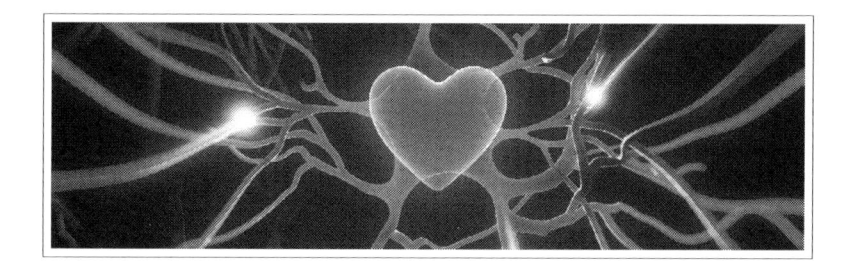

2.

ANS Response Patterns

As explored in the previous exercise, each person has both learned and habitual patterns of Autonomic Nervous System (ANS) activation, also called your Autonomic mode. People can be in various patterns of sympathetic over-dominance (overly stressed or up-regulated), parasympathetic over-dominance (overly depressed or down-regulated), in a nicely balanced mode between the two, or bouncing between the two with both operating at the same time. The sympathetic mode is known simplistically as the *'Fight or Flight'* mode. And the parasympathetic mode is often simplistically referred to as the *'Rest and Repose'* mode, or the *'Feeding and Fornicating'* mode, since it gets evoked during feeding and sexuality.

However, there is much more complexity in how you respond when in these various modes. There is a huge difference between fighting and flighting, and between resting, eating and fornicating or connecting deeply with others. Some people have habits and patterns of fighting and getting aggressive when stressed. Others tend to want to withdraw and do flighting or running away from the situation. Still others can rebound from stress, straight into a deep parasympathetic *'Freeze'* response, or else into such parasympathetic responses as those of *'Folding'* or *'Tending and Befriending'*.

It is incredibly useful to understand your patterns of ANS response to stressors. With awareness you begin to open up choice. The more you know about your patterns and your habitual unconscious responses and triggers, the greater the wisdom and freedom you can bring to your life. The following exercises will help you explore your ANS response patterns and provide useful information for you and your *m*BIT Coach to work with.

Facilitators Guide

As indicated in the previous section on ANS Mode, each of us has learned unconscious patterns and habits in ANS response and activation i.e. patterns of ANS mode that we typically operate in and from. Some people appear to be much more prone to sympathetic dominance and therefore more prone to experiencing stress, fight and flight responses. They are attuned to being stressed and to getting aroused and aggravated easily. Other people are more parasympathetic dominant in their typical responses to life; they are more chilled, or even somewhat depressed. Or they kick quickly into depression in response to the challenges or exigencies of life. And while your overall ANS mode is important, so too is your specificity of response to stressors. Whether you do fight, flight, freeze, fold or some other response to stress makes a huge difference to the results you get in any situation.

Your Client's ANS Response is really key to how they cope with life, to how they respond to their world (and thereby create their reality) and to the sorts of competencies they can bring to any situation. As shown in *mBraining*, the competencies and functions that the Client's multiple brains (head, heart and gut) operate in are influenced and determined by what their ANS is doing. They can't respond in a relaxed manner, with a heart filled with joy, if they are massively stressed and in sympathetic fight or flight mode. Equally they can't respond attentively and bring a joy for life and an open-minded curiosity to a situation if they are massively depressed and in parasympathetic '*freeze*' rebound.

So in this exercise your Client will examine their ANS response patterns, and working with you, this will become a powerful area for *m*BIT Coaching. Using this you'll help them overcome old un-useful patterns and in their place open up new possibilities in how they respond and orient to the stressors of life.

Exploring Your ANS Response Patterns

This section explores the patterns of Autonomic response your Client does habitually when impacted by a stressor, either acute or chronic. This provides you and the Client with insights into their default preferences and habits and how they respond to stressors in their world and opens up avenues to do *m*BIT Coaching processes to bring more wisdom to their choices and patterns.

> *Do you have any overall or repeated patterns of Autonomic Nervous System (ANS) response in your life? For example, in stressful, threatening or challenging situations do you typically 'Fight' (e.g. become angry and defensive), or 'Flight' (e.g. withdraw or run away), or do you usually 'Freeze' (e.g. shutdown), or perhaps 'Fold' (e.g. capitulate and give in), or do you prefer to 'Tend and Befriend' (e.g. focus on bonding with other people and maintaining relationships with them)?*

As a generalization, research indicates that men and women typically show different response to stressors. Men are often more inclined to fight or flight responses, whereas women typically try to bond more and improve their relationships. [For example see Mather & Lighthall, 2012; Podsiadło & Urbanik et al., 2011; or Wang & Korczykowski et al., 2007]. However, each person is unique and different, and can have a range of varying responses. Where one person may start out with a flight response, when further threatened they may then become angry and start to fight. Another person may do the reverse, start out angry and ready to fight and if further challenged, then freeze or run away.

What's important in this exercise is to get the Client to explore and examine their usual patterns and what their outcome is in using these patterns. Help them explore whether the patterns serve them, or indeed, how the patterns affect the ecology of their life and their relationships (both with others and themselves), their health, etc. Look for the secondary gains (hidden benefits and consequences) and explore with your Client wiser ways to achieve these.

References:

Mather, M. & Lighthall, N. R., *Risk and Reward Are Processed Differently in Decisions Made Under Stress*, Current Directions in Psychological Science, 21 (1): 36, 2012.

Podsiadło, L. & Urbanik, A. et al., *Functional Magnetic Resonance Imaging of Different Genders in the Activation of Brain Emotional Centers*, Iranian Journal of Radiology, Volume: 8; Issue: S1; p. 82, 2011.

Wang, J. & Korczykowski, M. et al., *Gender difference in neural response to psychological stress*, Social Cognitive and Affective Neuroscience, 05/2007; 2(3):227-39, 2007.

> *In what contexts, situations or degrees of stress would you typically:*

Fight?

Flight?

Freeze?

Fold/Capitulate?

Tend and Befriend?

This question investigates the various strategies your Client does for how they respond to stress. Help them explore their strengths and weaknesses with these strategies. You are looking to enable greater wisdom, flexibility and choice in how they respond to stressors. The first step of course is awareness, so explore their answers to the above question and the various contexts and strategies in depth. Do they have issues with inappropriate anger for example? Do they always respond by freezing? Are they able to move from one strategy to another as appropriate? Were they aware of these patterns and do they serve them? Work through each of their strategies using the *m*BIT Roadmap to determine what each brain is attempting to achieve in its response to the stressor, and find ways to align the brains around a set of responses that are a higher expression of the person. Explore with your Client how they can bring more Compassion, Creativity and Courage to their responses to stress and the above situations and contexts. Explore emergent outcomes with them and ways to achieve those.

> *Are there contexts, people or situations in which your responses listed above do not serve you wisely or you could handle more generatively and wisely? How does this impact your life and your sense of self?*

This question explores more deeply the impacts and ecology of the Client's responses to stressors. It opens them up to outcomes and personal responsibility and to thinking through the systemic impacts their behavior has on their lives, their relationships and their sense of identity. Help your Client to explore these deeply. The more your Client realizes the impacts on their life and their way of being and becoming, the more they'll be willing to make changes and take on new options. The information you glean from this question can be very fruitful for doing *m*BIT Coaching up the Roadmap and especially for exploring the applications of the Highest Expressions to these aspects of the Client's ways of living and doing.

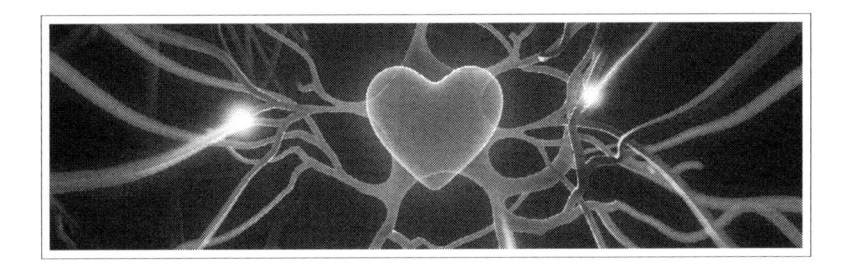

3.
Neural Syntax (Brain) Patterns

As a generalization, people have patterns or preferences in how they filter the world, how they utilize their neural networks or *'brains'* and how they integrate or process their experience through their head, heart and gut brains.

We all know someone who is *'all heart'*, the person who always leads with their heart-based emotions, who focuses primarily (either positively or negatively) on connecting with others, or on dreams, values and their heart's-desires. We say that people like this are *'people people'* and they often *'wear their hearts on their sleeves'*. Their lives, decisions and actions are always heartfelt.

On the other hand, I'm sure you know someone who is *'super-logical'*, who lives through logic, through always over-thinking, through language and through their head brain. Such people are often very dissociated from their emotions, from their heart, and can also be disconnected from their gut-based intuitions. If it isn't logical, then they just won't do it.

Then there's the gutsy people, the ones predominantly connected with their visceral feelings of intuition and courage. They take action and think about it later. They're gung-ho. Logic isn't their strong point, and often neither are the sensitive emotions of love and compassion. They are the action heroes. No fear. Their motto is *'no pain, no gain!'*

While the above descriptions are characterizations, and very few people fit those descriptions in all contexts of life, they nevertheless resound because we've all met people who fit the moulds we've just described. But most people are a bit more well-rounded than that. And the reason is that while people have a pattern or preference for which brain they tend to use as the primary neural network to process, filter and respond to life, we all tend to then have a secondary and tertiary preference for which brain next adds into the process.

In the field of *m*BIT this sequence of brain use is called the neural syntax. This is the sequence, or *'syntax'*, by which we construct our experience and reality. We make meaning and sense of our world by using our various brains to process our experience. For some people this pattern involves typically processing with the heart first, then the head and then the gut. For others it might be head then gut, and the heart doesn't even get a look-in. We are all different, and our patterns can also be contextual. But we definitely all have our habitual patterns and preferences. And how you use your brains, the sequence of how they communicate and integrate together, makes a massive difference to the results you create.

So in this exercise you'll explore your preferred patterns of brain use and neural syntax. You can do this for a particular context, or as an overall pattern in your life. Your preference for the sequence in which you use your brains provides you with strengths and weaknesses, so it's quite powerful and instructive to uncover your habitual patterns and preferences for this.

Facilitators Guide

Once your Client has determined their Neural Syntax (or brain) preference – their pattern of preferred sequence of using their multiple brains – whether it's an overall pattern that is generalized across their life, or only in a specific context, you then need to assist and coach them to learn to bring their patterns into balance. For wisdom and the most adaptive or generative response in life, they need to be able to use all their brains, to bring their least preferred brains into play, to strengthen them and give them focus, salience and value. It's just like with muscles, if you don't use a muscle then over time it weakens and atrophies. To be strong and healthy overall, your Client needs to build all their muscles and use them together appropriately. The neural networks and pathways are the same. Indeed, the work in neuroscience on what is called *'neuro-genesis'* or the growth of new neuronal cells, synapses and networks, shows that with valued use and appropriate stimulation you can grow new neuronal connections and pathways in all three brains.

Strengthen via the Highest Expressions

One of the most powerful ways to balance and strengthen the weakest brain preference is to use the Highest Expressions of the non-dominant brain(s). By using the Highest Expressions you can exercise your Client's under-developed neural functions in an optimal and adaptive way. This is powerful and beneficial because:

- Highest Expressions are integrative across brains and require all of the brains to work together

- Highest Expressions are integrative across the Prime Functions within the brain they are operating in and so exercise all the functions of the neural network

Brain Preferences

On a scale of 0 to 5, where 0 is no skill (or no perceived use or preference) whatsoever, and 5 represents the most skill you can imagine (or most perceived use or preference), rate yourself in how much facility you have with each of your brains (head, heart, gut).

This is about determining, at a broad-brush level, which of the Neural Networks or brains is strongest and what the Client perceives their levels of skills or preferences are with each. You can also get the Client to utilize the survey tool available at mbraining.com for a more detailed examination of their preferences for each brain.

Head (place a circle or X below to rate your level of skill and competence)

(No Skill) **0 - - - - - 1 - - - - - 2 - - - - - 3 - - - - - 4 - - - - - 5** (Magnificent Skill)
(or preference)   (or preference)

Heart (place a circle or X below to rate your level of skill and competence)

(No Skill) **0 - - - - - 1 - - - - - 2 - - - - - 3 - - - - - 4 - - - - - 5** (Magnificent Skill)
(or preference)   (or preference)

Gut (place a circle or X below to rate your level of skill and competence)

(No Skill) **0 - - - - - 1 - - - - - 2 - - - - - 3 - - - - - 4 - - - - - 5** (Magnificent Skill)
(or preference)   (or preference)

❓ *Sequence: Do you have a preferred sequence in which you use your brains e.g. do you prefer to use your heart first and then your head, or your head first and then your gut etc.? (You might find it useful in answering this question to remember and revisit some specific instances in which you have recently made a decision.)*

This question explores the sequence the Client believes they typically use. Their answer here is likely to match the sequence of scores from the first part of the exercise (or the results from the online *m*BIT Brain Preference Survey tool). Note that brain preference and sequence can be contextual, the Client may use different patterns at work compared to home etc. If the Client's response to this sequence question doesn't match the sequence shown in the first part of the exercise, then explore this mismatch with them. It's about bringing awareness of their (usually) unconscious patterns and preferences to conscious awareness and thereby to choice.

❓ *Contexts: Are there specific contexts or situations in which you prefer to use one brain over another or one sequence over another? How does this impact your life? What benefits or disadvantages does it bring you?*

Our strengths can often become our weakness. And overuse of any pattern can become a problem. Equally, every pattern while having benefits also has drawbacks and limitations. If you always use your heart first, you'll be strongly connected to values, strongly connected to other people and able to feel deep emotions. However, you'll also be likely to be swayed by emotion over logic (head) and at times may be too swamped by your emotions to take appropriate action (gut).

So this question allows you to explore with your Client the systemic impacts of their patterns and preferences in using their multiple brains. Help them understand where and how their patterns serve them, and more importantly, where and how their patterns limit their success in life. Use the *m*BIT Roadmap and Highest Expressions to uncover wiser ways for them to stretch themselves, to be more creative in their patterns and preferences and to have the courage to do new ways of *mBraining* their life.

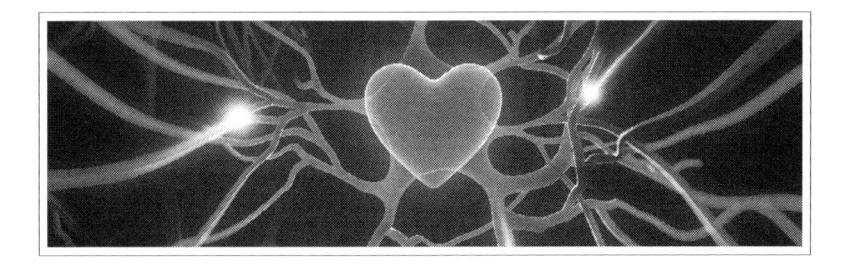

4.
Neural Integration Constraint Patterns

Behavioral modeling research in the field of *m*BIT has uncovered that there are five major classes of issues that arise for people when their brains are not aligned or integrated fully. These are known as *m*BIT Integration Constraints and are ways in which you may inappropriately utilize your head, heart and gut intelligences so that you create problems in achieving the success and happiness you desire in life.

Processes that limit or constrain multiple brain integration:

1. When one intelligence is used to the exclusion of the others

2. When one intelligence swamps or overrides the others

3. When one intelligence is used inappropriately to do the job or prime function of the others

4. When one or more of the three intelligences are in conflict or antagonism with each other

5. When the intelligences are working together but are used in the '*wrong*' sequence for achieving the outcome

Probably one of the easiest ways to determine if you suffer from one or more of the above constraints is if you see evidence in your life of non-alignment of your brains. Look through the following list to see if any relate to you.

*m*BIT Non-Alignment Indicators

The clues that will alert you when your brains are not aligned or integrated:

- You experience internal conflict between your thoughts, feelings and actions
- You've not acted upon your dreams, goals and plans
- You do unwanted behaviors or habits and don't know why or have difficulty in stopping
- You find it difficult to make a decision(s)
- Something within you is making it difficult for you to motivate yourself to take action
- You sabotage yourself from achieving your goals

Facilitators Guide

Determining NIC's is not an easy task for someone not trained in *m*BIT, so with this exercise you may have to first educate your Client in what each of the NIC's looks like using examples that pertain to their life and make sense to them. Perhaps start the exercise with the Client under your guidance and then leave them to continue working on it in their own time between coaching sessions.

Note however that the patterns of Neural Integration Constraints that a Client has in their life are truly vital areas for *m*BIT Coaching. If your Client continually uses one of their brains to the exclusion or override of the others then this will continue to create problems and issues in their life. Teasing out these patterns and then educating your Client in using all of their neural networks, and in the most appropriate sequence for the outcome (and typically this will be the Foundational Sequence) will be a truly important generative process that will echo across the contexts of their life.

In debriefing this exercise, look for corresponding patterns between the NIC's highlighted in this section and the Neural Syntax Patterns and brain preferences uncovered in the previous section. It's likely that there will be overlaps and correlations between these various preferences and patterns, and this will help you show your Client how their habitual preferences and their perceived strengths when overused or used inappropriately can actually become a weakness and cause ongoing issues in their life. For example, someone who has a preference in using their Heart brain to filter their world and direct their decisions may end up swamping the other brains with the messages and directives from the heart. This can then cause them to have (do) internal conflict and to end up sabotaging their outcomes when the head and gut derail their actions and focus.

Ultimately what we are after in *m*BIT Coaching is to assist people to gain more freedom, choice and flexibility. Becoming aware of how overused strengths turn into limiting behaviors helps convince the Client to start exercising and building skills in using the less preferred neural networks. Greater levels of wisdom come from greater choice and skill in using all three brains, in appropriate and finely nuanced ways, and through balance, alignment and appropriate sequence.

Exploring your Neural Integration Patterns

> *Are there specific times, contexts or situations in which you experience internal conflict between your thoughts, feelings and actions? How specifically does this play out? Are there any patterns with this? And how does this impact your life?*

We all have times when we experience conflict between head, heart and gut, however if there are recurring patterns with this then it is a fruitful area for alignment and *m*BIT Coaching. So the key with this exercise is to explore patterns of internal conflict with respect to neural integration, and to look for the triggers, secondary gains (hidden benefits) and overused competencies or missing skills that are the underlying causes. Once you and the Client know *'how'* they are creating the internal conflicting and what patterns of brain use are involved, you can then guide them in wiser ways of using their mind-body and their multiple brains to resolve and dissolve any *'conflicting'*. One of the key things you are looking for in their answers to the above questions are the NIC's that are in play and the patterns of constraining that the Client does with unconscious competence – then re-skill them to having more choice in neural integration between the brains.

> *Are there specific times, contexts or situations in which you have not acted upon your dreams, goals and plans? What are the details of this and what are the patterns you see in your life with this? How does this impact your life?*

There are many ways in which someone could stop themselves from acting on dreams, goals and outcomes, and they mostly all involve specific ways or constraints on how a person uses their multiple brains. You could either not fill your heart and mind with compelling and joyfully desired dreams and goals or you could dishearten yourself and thereby discourage yourself by using your head brain to think of ways in which your dreams and goals might be thwarted or cause you problems. You might hold great dreams in your heart, but then focus on fear of change at a gut level and thereby block yourself from taking action. So the key to using the Client's answers to the above questions is to explore the NIC's involved in how they specifically thwart themselves in acting upon their dreams and goals. And in particular look for patterns of this across contexts and situations. If you find patterns of unconscious skill in how they are using their multiple brains to constrain their success, then work with them to build new skills and resources, new ways to move forward, new ways to interrupt the old patterns and instead do more generative responding in their life.

Are there specific times, contexts or situations in which you do unwanted behaviors or habits and don't know why or have difficulty in stopping? How specifically does this play out? And how does this impact your life?

Compulsions, addictions and dysfunctional habits are often driven by insatiable hungers and desires and the use of one brain to do the job of another. When someone tries for example to *'eat until their heart is content'*, this is the gut and heart doing each other's Prime Functions and creating a loop that can never be satiated properly. We discuss compulsions in Chapter 8 of *mBraining* and will also examine them in the *m*BIT Toolkit exercises in this Workbook. Compulsive behaviors and habits that the Client has trouble controlling are important areas for *m*BIT Coaching and for bringing balanced ANS mode and Highest Expression to.

Are there specific times, contexts or situations in which you find it difficult to make a decision(s)? How specifically does this play out? What are the patterns in this? How does this impact your life?

Decisions are best made when in balanced ANS mode and using all three brains, aligned and in optimum sequence. Constraint patterns in how the Client does their decision strategies will lead to difficulties and problems in the decision process. Do they over-think the decision and ignore their heart? Do they kick into a focus on gut-based fear? Do they ignore the messages from one of their brains? Explore the Client's patterns with this and then coach them in a wiser and more generative process using the skills from the *m*BIT Toolkit that deal with decision-making (in Chapter 8 of *mBraining*).

> *Are there specific times, contexts or situations in which something within you makes it difficult for you to motivate yourself to take action? How specifically does this play out? And how does this impact your life?*

If a person gets disheartened they are likely to become discouraged. If they focus on problems or invest way too much time in loops in their head over-thinking a situation, then they'll distract themselves or demotivate themselves from getting started or taking action. Look for the patterns in how the Client is doing their motivation strategies, for how they are using their multiple brains to take action in life. Then coach them in wiser and more useful ways of using their neurology and the resources of the Prime Functions of each of their brains as well as the appropriate use of their ANS to build energy and excitement for getting started and then flow for keeping on moving.

> *Are there specific times, contexts or situations in which you sabotage yourself from achieving your goals? How specifically do you do this? Are there any patterns in this? How does this impact your life?*

Self-sabotage comes in many forms. There's fear of success and fear of failure, both seemingly different, but often driven from the same underlying issues. Explore the stories and narratives your Client is running in their head, and search for the NIC's involved in their sabotage strategies. It's a skill to be able to repeatedly snatch defeat from the jaws of success, so bring the patterns of unconscious competency to conscious awareness and choice for the Client. Then coach them in wiser emergent ways of doing Highest Expressing in their lives.

> *Are there specific times, contexts or situations in which one of your intelligences or brains is used to the exclusion of the others? What are the details of this? What are the patterns? And how does this impact your life?*

This section is more explicit about the specific NIC and how it plays out in the Client's life. It's also likely to relate closely to the Client's Neural Syntax preferences explored in the previous section. It can be very impactful for the Client to gain awareness in how their preferences are both generating success and challenges in their life. So explore these patterns and their impacts with your Client and coach them to gain more wisdom and ecological choice.

> *Are there specific times, contexts or situations in which one of your intelligences or brains swamps or overrides the others? What are the details of this? What are the patterns? And how does this impact your life?*

Again, this section is more explicit about the specific NIC and how it plays out in the Client's life. As per the previous point, it's also likely to relate closely to the Client's Neural Syntax preferences explored in the previous section. If one of the brains is swamping the others, there is likely a reason, or pattern of reasons for why it is doing that and what the overall system is trying to achieve with what it currently knows. Exploring this pattern and helping the Client bring the other brains into clearer communication and into a more equal relationship, so that swamping is no longer an issue, will have amazing impacts on the Client's life.

> *Are there specific times, contexts or situations in which one of your intelligences or brains is used inappropriately to do the job or Prime Function of the others? What are the details of this? What are the patterns? And how does this impact your life?*

Humans are incredibly complex and adaptable organisms, and neural networks can learn to do all sorts of behaviors and processes. So it's not surprising that sometimes, depending on life history, a Client can end up with one of their brains doing the job of another. But this can cause major issues in life. In one example, a young woman whose heart had been broken, decided never to trust her heart again, for anything, and from that moment forth started using her gut brain to do the heart's tasks of valuing and relational affect. Not only did she now treat everyone and everything as if it was food and thereby consumed life, she also ended up massively over-eating and went from being a very slender and healthy individual to being morbidly obese and plagued with major health issues. Getting her to realize that this had become her pattern and coaching her to learn to trust her heart again, especially when it's messages were integrated in a balanced and wise way, allowed her to once again find ways of relating to people and objects in an ecological manner and not as items to be consumed.

> *Are there specific times, contexts or situations in which one or more of your intelligences or brains are in conflict or antagonism with each other? What are the details of this? What are the patterns? And how does this impact your life?*

This is about skills in criteria and outcome alignment. The Client is able to have their multiple brains communicate with one another, and all are in play, but the Client doesn't have the unconscious skills in negotiating between the brains so they can incorporate each others requirements. Coaching the Client up the *m*BIT Roadmap and bringing their awareness (and skill level) to this important process will help them generalize it into their life and their relationship with themselves and with others.

> *Are there specific times, contexts or situations in your intelligences or brains are working together but are used in the wrong sequence? What are the details of this? What are the patterns? And how does this impact your life?*

As we know, sequence counts. If you change the sequence, you can often markedly change the results. And not every situation requires the same sequence. So while we have found in *m*BIT that the Foundational Sequence is a great place to start, you still need to be sensitive and flexible in finding the most appropriate sequence for your Client and their situation. Most importantly this exercise is about examining and exploring the patterns of this NIC in the person's life. Do they use the same sequence over and over and in ways that create problems for them? If so, coach them in finding more useful ways and bringing greater choice and requisite variety to the ways they use their multiple brains.

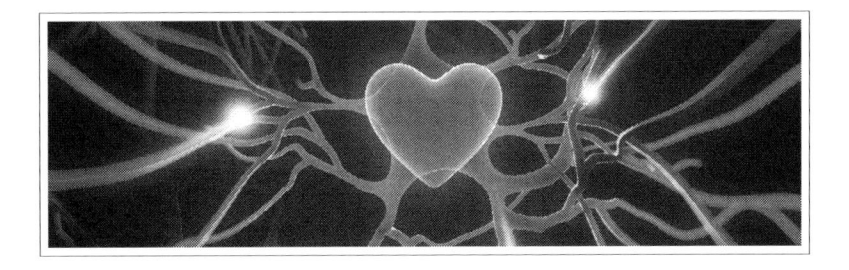

5.

Neural Communication Patterns

Communication is all about listening to the feedback from *and* between the brains, and is a required component for building trust. If one brain refuses to communicate with another or stonewalls and ignores the communication it's receiving, this quickly destroys trust. Communication is about listening and sharing. Always listen with respect to every message that comes from each of your multiple brains and acknowledge them. The messages are important and provide valuable information you disregard at your peril. As a wise person once told us, "*the facts are our friends.*"

From an *mBraining* perspective, it helps to remember that each neural network communicates its unique form of '*facts*' based on its prime functions and particular mode of communication. It's important that each brain works harmoniously with each other's '*facts*' and you are sensitive to each brain's unique language and method of communication.

The following lists indicate some of the ways in which the brains communicate and which you can use to begin to become aware of your own patterns and preferences for brain communication and signaling.

The Head communicates via:

- ☺ Internal dialogue
- ☺ Internal sounds
- ☺ Internal images
- ☺ Internal Kinesthesia (feelings)
- ☺ Dreams, symbols, visions, words, narratives, metaphor

The Heart communicates via:

- ♥ Emotions and feelings
- ♥ Interest, attention and salience
- ♥ Symbolic images, dreams and visions
- ♥ Kinesthetic sensations e.g. pain, tightness, warmth etc.
- ♥ Beats, rhythm
- ♥ Speed, timing of movements
- ♥ Breathing
- ♥ Tones (music, song)
- ♥ Quiet/small voice and simple words
- ♥ Heart-based language
- ♥ Smells
- ♥ Heart-related health issues
- ♥ *'Felt-sense'* and body/chest sensations
- ♥ Electrical signals

The Gut communicates via:

- Hungers, lusts, cravings for foods and satiety signals
- Motivation signals and visceral feelings of attraction, compulsion and repulsion
- Fear signals and visceral feelings of safety and threat e.g. fear, apprehension, foreboding, nagging, etc.
- Peristalsis — swallowing, choking, burping, vomiting, flatulence, excreting
- Kinesthetic/gut visceral sensations e.g. anxiety, butterflies in the stomach, cramping, gut rumblings, unsettled stomach, heartburn, etc.
- Physical movement (including physical hesitation)
- Gut/GIT health issues, immune system issues
- Diaphragmatic breathing
- Belly laughing
- Guttural sounds & simple words
- Quiet/small voice and simple words
- Gut-based language
- Tastes/smells
- Moral disgust and physical disgust, distaste and stench/dis-smell
- *'Felt-sense'* and body/torso sensations
- Dreams/visions

The brains also communicate via *'Gateways'*, these are points of co-innervation (shared nerve connections) between the brains and points that you have both conscious control over as well as autonomic and unconscious connections to. By tracking for signals and feelings in these areas you can often determine when the brains are communicating to you via these gateways. For example, a common experience is to have a *'lump in the throat'* or a feeling of stuckness in the throat area. People say things like, *"I just can't swallow that idea"*, *"This issue sticks in my throat"*, *"It bought a lump to my throat"* – these are all neuro-linguistic indicators of communication from the gut brain to the head brain. The gut brain is tracking for threat and is expressing a message that the issue is not something it can digest or swallow. Since the whole of the esophagus is co-innervated by both the gut brain and the head brain, the gut can control the motor and sensory nerves in the throat and clearly communicate to the head (and to your conscious mind) that it has something to say about the issue.

mBraining Communication Gateways

The bridges or gateways through which conscious communication and control can occur:

1. The face
2. The tongue and throat
3. The hands
4. The diaphragm and intercostals
5. The pelvic floor
6. The feet

In the following exercises you'll explore how your brains communicate with you. Research shows that the more attuned and aware you are of the messages and communication signals from your heart and gut brains, the greater the level of intuitions and inner wisdom you'll be able to bring to your decisions and your life.

Facilitators Guide

"Learning implies a great sensitivity... How can there be a very alert, clear mind if the organism itself is dull and heavy?"

Krishnamurti

Learning and change require a nuanced sensory attentiveness and sensitivity (sense-it-ivity) to the signals and messages coming from the intelligences in the body (the heart and gut brains, the ANS, etc.) Being able to communicate with your multiple brains and being aware of the communication signals from the brains are key competencies needed for integration, alignment and wisdom. For example, as described in *mBraining*, a study published recently in the journal Psychological Science, shows that intuition from hunches and listening to your heart can assist in decision-making, but the quality of this can vary from individual to individual (Dunn & Galton et al., 2010). The research shows that trustworthiness of intuition is strongly influenced by what is happening physically in our bodies and how attuned we are to this.

Listening to the heart

To investigate how different bodily reactions influence decision-making, Dr. Barnaby Dunn, of the Brain Sciences Unit in Cambridge, England and his co-authors asked study participants to learn how to win at a card game they had never played before. The game was designed so there were no obvious strategies to follow and instead players had to follow their hunches and intuition. While playing the game, each participant wore a heart rate monitor and a sensor that measured the amount of sweat on their fingertips. Most players gradually found a way to win at the game and reported having relied on intuition rather than reason. Subtle changes in the players' heart rates and sweat responses affected how quickly they learned to make the best choices.

Interestingly, the quality of the advice their bodies gave them varied. Some people's instincts were spot on and they mastered the game quickly. Other people's bodies told them exactly the wrong moves to make and they learned slowly or never found a way to win. Dunn and his co-authors found the link between hunches and intuitive decision-making to be stronger in people who were more aware of their own heartbeat. So for some individuals being able to '*listen to their heart*' helped them make wiser choices.

What's even more important from Dunn's research is that in a second study, subjects were instructed to listen to and attend to their heartbeats and this increased the success in tuning into their intuitions and ability to master the game. As indicated by Dr. Dunn, "What happens in our bodies really does appear to influence what goes on in our minds."

Other studies on what is known as '*interoceptive awareness*' (the awareness of bodily states, usually measured by awareness of heartbeat, see for example, Pollatos, Gramann & Schandry, 2007) have shown that the perception of bodily states is a crucial determinant for the processing and subjective experience of feelings. The greater the ability to track the signals from the heart and body, the more a person can deeply experience feelings and emotions. This extends to the ability to do empathy and compassion. For example, a study by Ernst and Northoffet (2012) found that increasing awareness of heartbeat supports greater empathy and shows up as increased activity in the brain circuits used during empathy.

And in one truly fascinating study, Dr. Blas Couto and colleagues at the University of Cambridge (2013) explored the impacts of changes to interoceptive awareness in a male patient "*with two hearts*". The 32-year-old man had a heart condition and was awaiting a heart transplant, but in the meantime was fitted with a mechanical pump to aid his failing left ventricle. The researchers found that the '*Man with two hearts*' awareness of his heartbeat was dominated by the input produced by the artificial pump and the results from social and emotional tests showed that compared with normal controls, he exhibited impairments in empathy, theory of mind (representing other people's mental states), and decision-making tasks. However, he demonstrated otherwise normal performance on tests of intelligence, language and memory.

What all this means

What all these intriguing research findings mean for you as an *m*BIT Coach is that if you have a Client who exhibits little connection with their feelings or can't tap into the signals from their heart, then you can get them to practice tuning into their heartbeat and this will build interoceptive awareness and over time strengthen their ability to connect with their heart and gut brains. Communication requires awareness, so start them off with daily practice of just 5 minutes per day listening to and feeling their heartbeat.

Amplifying the signals with touch

> *"When you begin to touch your heart...You begin to discover how much warmth and gentleness is there, as well as how much space."*
>
> Pema Chödrön

Work by Professor Kristin Neff in the field of Self-Compassion shows that holding your hands to your heart and doing compassionate self-caring leads to the release of the love and bonding neuro-hormone oxytocin, decreases the stress hormone cortisol and helps alleviate depression and anxiety. There is also a growing body of research (for example see Madan & Singhal, 2012) on the impact of touch and gestures and their ability to influence neurophysiology including heart rate, cardiac vagal tone, emotion, memory and other mind-body states. So it's not surprising that in our recent modeling work and *m*BIT action research we have found that touching your heart region for example has a very noticeable and real effect and strengthens feelings of compassion in the heart. We've found that getting Clients to touch whatever region or brain they are attempting to communicate with and get signals from, helps strongly facilitate those messages.

And there appears to be a significant difference to the quality and type of messages evoked by different forms of touch. The way a person touches their heart, gut or head seems to directionalize the experience towards differing Prime Functions. For example, (and you might want to try this for yourself right now), holding an opened hand or hands over your heart as you think of an issue typically evokes the Prime Functions of relational affect and connection with others. Whereas, holding your hand(s) as a fist over your heart appears to stimulate a focus on values. This is contrasted with touching a finger (or multiple fingers) to your heart, as if pointing to it, which seems to bring forth emotions related to the situation. And the experience changes by using the left hand versus the right hand, versus both hands. Try it for yourself, it's subtle yet powerful. And works with heart, gut and head brains.

So you can powerfully help your Client to really get in touch with the communication of their multiple brains by getting them to physically touch each region (using various gestures of open hands, closed hands and fingers) as they focus on signals and messages from that region.

Giving your Client a '*taste*' for the messages from their brains

Professor Eugene Gendlin (2010) in his work on communicating with the '*felt sense*' of the body says that it can be thought of as a taste. And since taste and felt visceral sense are important ways in which the gut brain communicates with the head brain, you could task your Client with learning to educate and improve their ability to notice and make refined distinctions in taste. As they become attuned to this sensory experience in their lives, they are more likely to begin to notice the messages of taste (and smell) being presented to them by their gut and heart brains and thereby begin to make greater distinctions on their felt sense. In terms of increasing awareness and skills in smell, you can task your Client with learning about smells and fragrances. There are aromatherapy kits and wine appreciation kits that can be bought and used to educate the sense of smell for example.

ANS Mode and Smell

Another interesting and useful distinction to be aware of is that ANS mode can influence how our brains process odors and smells – when we are stressed the world '*stinks*'. Research by Professor Wen Li and colleagues, at the University of Wisconsin, found that people experiencing an increase in anxiety show a decrease in the perceived pleasantness of odors (Krusemark & Li et al., 2013). Smells become more negative as anxiety increases.

Two brain circuits that don't typically "talk" to each other – one linked to our sense of smell and another linked to emotional processing – can become cross-wired when we experience stress-induced anxiety. The result is that stressful experiences transform normally neutral odors into bad ones. According to Professor Li, "In typical odor processing, it is usually just the olfactory system that gets activated. But when a person becomes anxious, the emotional system becomes part of the olfactory processing stream."

The research team believes that this effect accumulates over time and the more anxiety that is experienced, the more the cross-wiring between the two brain circuits strengthens – resulting in more and more otherwise neutral smells turning into bad ones. The vicious cycle triggered by this effect is that the smells themselves begin to contribute to more anxiety.

Also note that in various spiritual traditions, smell is said to be strongly linked to the heart, and our behavioral modeling action research backs this up. So share this with your Clients and get them to start paying attention to odor signals. Ask them to track what things "smell like". Does an idea '*stink*', does a situation smell good or bad. This is a subtle but important way in which the heart and gut brains communicate with the head brain.

Using NIE's

Remember also to utilize Neural Integrative Engagements (NIE's) as described in Chapter 5 of *mBraining*. These help amplify and facilitate communication between the brains. Especially note the use and importance of processes like fasting. Research has shown that interoceptive awareness is increased by fasting (Herbert & Herbert, 2012), so by getting your Client to do a short fast (if medically appropriate) and at the same time paying attention to the signals and messages from their heart and gut, you can increase their ability and awareness of the communication from their multiple brains.

References:

Couto, Blas & Salles, Alejo et al., *The man who feels two hearts: the different pathways of interoception*, Social Cognitive Affective Neuroscience, July 24, 2013.

Dunn, Barnaby D. & Galton, Hannah C. et al., *Listening to Your Heart: How Interoception Shapes Emotion Experience and Intuitive Decision Making*, Psychological Science, vol. 21 no. 12 1835-1844, December 2010.

Ernst, Jutta & Northoffet, Georg et al., *Interoceptive Awareness Enhances Neural Activity During Empathy*, Human Brain Mapping 000:000–000, 2012.

Gendlin, Eugene, *Focusing*, Ebury Digital, 2010.

Herbert, Beate M. & Herbert, Cornelia et al., *Effects of short-term food deprivation on interoceptive awareness, feelings and autonomic cardiac activity*, Biological Psychology, Volume 89, Issue 1, Pages 71–79, January 2012.

Krusemark, Elizabeth A., Novak, Lucas R., Gitelman, Darren R. & Li, Wen, *When the Sense of Smell Meets Emotion: Anxiety-State-Dependent Olfactory Processing and Neural Circuitry Adaptation*, The Journal of Neuroscience, 33(39), 25 September 2013.

Madan, Christopher & Singhal, Anthony, *Using actions to enhance memory:effects of enactment, gestures and exercise on human memory*, Frontiers in Psychology, Volume3, Article 507, November 2012.

Neff, Kristin, *The Chemicals of Care: How Self-Compassion Manifests in Our Bodies*, HuffingtonPost, Web, http://www.huffingtonpost.com/kristin-neff/self-compassion_b_884665.html, 27 June 2011.

Pollatos, O., Gramann, K. & Schandry, R., *Neural Systems Connecting Interoceptive Awareness and Feelings*, Human Brain Mapping 28:9 – 18, 2007.

Exploring your Neural Communication Patterns

Take a moment, somewhere quiet, settle and start doing Balanced Breathing (6 seconds in, 6 seconds out). Once you are in balance, talk to your heart, ask it a question. Then begin to notice in what ways your heart intelligence communicates to you. What do you notice? Looking at the list on the previous page, can you get a sense of the communication processes that your heart is using to answer you? Do you hear a voice and words? If so, is it the same or different to the normal voice in your head? Do you hear sounds? Do you see colors, symbols or images? Do feel certain 'felt-sense' sensations in your chest or body? What do you notice and experience?

You may have to assist your Client to really start to attune and notice the modality and submodality differences they experience when their particular brains are communicating with them. You want to both increase their awareness and help them make more and more subtle distinctions. You also want to build their convincer with this, so that they learn to really trust that their brains can and do communicate with them in quite specific and important ways.

Remember that you can get your Client to use self-touch of their heart/chest region to bring awareness and focus to communication from the heart, and to experiment with different sorts of touch and gestures. Also, to increase their overall interoceptive awareness of somatic signals, the research described at the beginning of this section shows that attending to and tracking for heartbeat will increase a person's ability to tune into intuitions and messages from their heart intelligence.

Now still doing Balanced Breathing (6 seconds in, 6 seconds out), talk to your gut brain, ask it a question. Then also begin to notice in what ways your gut intelligence communicates to you. What do you notice? Looking at the list on the previous pages, can you get a sense of the communication processes that your gut is using to answer you? Do you hear a voice and words? If so, is it the same or different to the normal voice in your head? Do you hear sounds? Do you see colors, symbols or images? Do feel certain 'felt-sense' sensations in your torso or body? Is there gurgling, movements, feelings in your gut or up in your throat? Do you get a sense of taste in your mouth? What do you notice and experience?

The work of Alyce Sorokie (2008), author of *'Gut Wisdom: Understanding and Improving Your Digestive Health'*, may be of use and relevance here for helping your Client tap into the intuitive messages from their gut brain. Alyce has found that the gut brain communicates best when it feels that it is in a safe environment (this is not surprising given the Prime Functions of the gut brain) and that such an environment can be created by getting the Client to lay comfortably, in a quiet room, with what she calls a *'belly buddy'* placed over the gut region. The main criteria for a belly buddy are that it must weigh around 1 to 2 kg's (2 – 4 pounds in imperial measures), cover the majority of the gut region and be warmed. Alyce sells belly buddies from her website (www.gutwisdom.com), or you can create your own using a hot water bottle or *'hottie'* (a natural rubber bladder filled with hot water and often covered with a soft fabric sleeve). The main aim is to create a warm, weighted cover that sits over the gut and shields it so that it feels safe and secure.

Additionally, touch and massage are important ways to bring awareness and attention to the gut region and open up interoceptive awareness of this area. This can be especially useful for people who are armoring or holding onto deep traumas at the gut level and thereby blocking communication from the gut to the other brains. In a coming section you will work specifically with your Client on exercises to uncover their patterns of NIB'ing (Neural Integration Blocking). In any case, you should note and be aware that extended and deep massage of the gut can release deeply held issues and should only be performed by an appropriately trained somatic masseur therapist. This is discussed more fully in Chapter 4 and Chapter 6 of *mBraining*.

[Reference: Sorokie, Alyce, *Gut Wisdom: Understanding and Improving Your Digestive Health*, Career Press, 2008.]

Now talk to your head, ask it a question and begin to notice in what ways your head communicates to you. What do you notice? Looking at the list on the previous pages, can you get a sense of the communication processes your head is using to answer you? Do you hear a voice and words? If so, is it the same or different to the normal voice in your head? Do you hear sounds? Do you see colors, symbols or images? Do feel certain 'felt-sense' sensations in your head or body? What do you notice and experience?

Remember to suggest to your Client they utilize touching of their head to facilitate focus on this region. Holding the head in both hands, touching a finger to the temple region, tapping or touching the '*third eye*' (pineal gland region), or even holding an opened hand across the forehead, can evoke different sorts of signals and messages. Get your Client to experiment with this as they attend to the communications occurring in their head brain. You can also suggest that they use visualization and to breathe up into the head area, filling it with colors, images, symbols or whatever helps them bring attention to the head area.

With all of the above exercises you are aiming for attuning and educating your Client in making better refined distinctions and discriminations on how their brains communicate. The more skills and practice the Client brings to this, the greater the level of self-awareness and mindfulness they will achieve. This is a base set of foundational competencies that are required for greater wisdom'ing in life. So it's worth investing time and focus on building communication skills with their multiple brains.

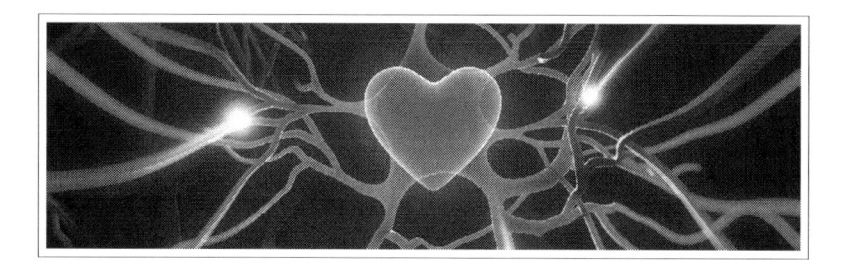

6.

*m*BIT Prime Functions

Your different brains have clearly distinct intelligences, prime functions and underlying core competencies. Each brain is optimized to perform very different functions. In the book '*mBraining*' we describe these in detail, but here we'll just summarize them.

The heart brain...

The heart is the seat of love and desires, goals, dreams and values. When you are connected to something you feel it and value it in your heart. When you hear that someone '*wears their heart on their sleeve*' you intuitively know that this does NOT mean that they are too logical. Instead, this is saying that they show their emotions, desires and intentions too obviously and readily.

If you say something is heartfelt, you aren't saying it's intellectually concise. And when you look at the language patterns of the heart, they express notions of love, connection, kindness and their converse. The prime functions of the heart intelligence involve salience, affection and relational issues such as a deep sense of truth and moral rightness as compared to rule based ethics.

HEART BRAIN PRIME FUNCTIONS

- **EMOTING** – emotional processing (e.g. anger, grief, hatred, joy, happiness etc.)
- **VALUES** – processing what's important to you and your priorities (and its relationship to the emotional strength of your aspirations, dreams, desires, etc.)
- **RELATIONAL AFFECT** – your felt connection with others (e.g. feelings of love/hate/indifference, compassion/uncaring, like/dislike, etc.)

The gut brain...

Due to its evolutionary history, the gut brain is responsible at a core level for determining what will be assimilated into self and excreted from self. It must determine what is required to maintain health and wellness in the system and decide whether molecules ingested into the stomach will be absorbed or excreted. Indeed, research has shown that more than 70 to 80 percent of our immune cells are located in the gut, and the enteric brain is intimately involved in managing immune function.

The prime functions of the gut are around protection, self-preservation, core identity and motility. Back when evolution was at the stage of complexity of sea cucumbers and worms, organisms only had a neural processing system of an enteric brain. This intelligence was used to detect threats and food in the environment and move away from danger and towards food. The gut brain maintains boundary detection and mobilization. In humans it is expressed as motivation, gutsy courage and a gut-felt desire to take action (or not).

GUT BRAIN PRIME FUNCTIONS

- **CORE IDENTITY** – a deep and visceral sense of core-self, and determining at the deepest levels what is '*self*' versus '*not-self*'
- **SELF-PRESERVATION** – protection of self, safety, boundaries, hungers and aversions
- **MOBILIZATION** – motility, impulse for action, gutsy courage and the will to act

The head brain...

In many ways the prime functions of the head brain are obvious, they involve the mental cognitive functions of logical thinking and include the processes of reasoning, perception and how we make meaning. Thought processes involve mental imagery, language expression, abstraction and symbol manipulation. The main job of the head is to intellectually make sense of the world and to provide executive control.

HEAD BRAIN PRIME FUNCTIONS

- **COGNITIVE PERCEPTION** – cognition, perception, pattern recognition, etc.
- **THINKING** – reasoning, abstraction, analysis, synthesis, meta-cognition etc.
- **MAKING MEANING** – semantic processing, languaging, narrative, metaphor, etc.

Facilitators Guide

This section on Prime Functions is designed to explore your Client's patterns of Prime Function skills and their use within each of their brains. You are looking for preferences, strengths, weaknesses, blockages and limitations. This will show where their *mBraining* map of the world is impoverished and provides points of leverage for bringing greater flexibility, requisite variety and control to their lives.

For example, if a Client has little skill in relational affect, then this is a vital area for *m*BIT Coaching, and change at this level can open up major areas of growth and new ways of being and action in their world. And since the Highest Expressions (of Compassion, Creativity and Courage) are integrative across Prime Functions (i.e. they require all Prime Functions to be in play), your Client's abilities to do the Highest Expressions will depend on having skills in and across all Prime Functions.

When you find a Prime Function that the Client has challenges, difficulties or a scotoma (blind-spot) with, then this can become a focus for the *m*BIT Coaching process. At this point, run the issue through the Highest Expressions Foundational Sequence and explore what emerges when the wisdom of the Client's aligned brains becomes focused on this. By feeding the pattern of the system back into itself, you create powerful ripples and generative opportunities for change in the Client's world modeling.

Additionally, strengths can become weaknesses; we can over-use them, or sometimes get lazy and under-utilize them. So take note of the Client's strengths in and across the Prime Functions and then explore whether they are using their strengths as a crutch, as a way to filter all their behaviors and processes through the same way of *mBraining*. Do they have strengths in say, motility and gutsy action, and now they over use that strength and bring it to bear in all situations of their life? In this case you now have a useful domain of enquiry to explore with them, to run through the *mBIT* Coaching process to see what their heart, head and gut thinks and feels about this. You can then task them with finding other ways to stretch themselves, to find new and more creative ways to achieve their outcomes and bring even more choice and flexibility to their life.

Exploring Your Heart Brain Prime Functions

This section explores how your Client is embracing their world at the level of heart and in what ways they may be limiting themselves with heart brain Prime Functions. This provides you and the Client with avenues to expand and evolve their heart intelligence to embrace greater skills in the Prime Functions of the heart and how they are *'en-heartening'* their life.

> *Emoting: Are there any heart-based emotions that challenge you or that you have blocks or difficulties with? For example, emotions you either can't feel or lack in your life? Or ones that take over and you don't have as much control with that you'd like to? Are there any specific contexts or situations that relate to these?*

Here you'll find if there are strengths (in particular looking for over-used or under-used strengths) or weaknesses in how the Client does emoting. Look for recurring patterns that may have generalized across contexts in the person's life. You can then explore them with the Client and run them through the *m*BIT Coaching processes to determine if the Client can emerge wiser ways of doing their heart based emoting.

> *Relational Affect: Do you have any blocks, challenges or difficulties with connecting with others, or building bonds of affection, friendship or deep loving? Do you have any issues with trust? Are there people or contexts that impact your ability to connect with and relate to others?*

None of us live in isolation, we all need to connect to and work with others in our lives. Indeed, we are largely brought into being and defined by our relatings with others. So this Prime Function is a deeply important one and deserves a lot of time and exploration. What are the patterns by which the Client connects with, or doesn't connect with, other people? In what contexts does this change? How do they relate with others? Can they feel empathy and oneness with others? Do they embrace deep love and bonding with others? With whom? And NOT with whom? Why? How?

Help them open up their heart and find ways to safely connect with themselves and others. Connection with others starts with connection with self. "*As within, so without.*" If the heart cannot love, appreciate and connect with the other brains, if there is no trust between the heart, head and gut, then the person will not easily be able to connect deeply with other hearts and minds. Remember that in *m*BIT we know that '*the heart leads*', so really invest a lot of time and value in helping your Client become very skillful in this Prime Function.

> ***Values:** Do you know what's important to you? Do you have a clear set of values? Do you have dreams and goals that make your heart sing? If not, how are you stopping or limiting yourself?*

Is the Client clear about what's important in their life? Do they use their heart wisely to determine what's valued and '*dear to their heart*'? Or are they tracking values at only a head level (espoused values)? Or perhaps representing values inappropriately as hungers at a gut level?

Note that there's a valid difference between '*Desire Values*' and '*Needs Values*'. Desires are those things we hold predominantly in the heart, we want them, we desire them, but we don't need them to survive. Needs values on the other hand are those things that are core to our identity, make us who we are, and are needed for our survival, either physically, emotionally or semantically. The majority of needs are also represented as desires, but they don't have to be. For example many people need to work, but may not desire or truly have heartfelt joy for work. On the other hand, you may value travel at a heart level, but it may not be a core need for you, if you don't travel then it won't threaten you at a gut level.

The idea with this exercise is to explore your Client's values and look for congruence, clarity and alignment. Do they use their heart appropriately to track for and sort their dreams, goals, desires and heart values? Are all their needs values also heart-based desire values? If not, do some *m*BIT Coaching around this. For example, if work is a needs value and yet is also not a desire value, then this is a fruitful avenue for coaching, to help your Client explore and emerge greater wisdom in finding work, or finding ways to engage with and perceive work, so that it satisfies and evokes both needs and heartfelt joy. You want to coach the Client to bring their world alive, to tap into the intelligence of vibrant heart valuing, to make effective use of this important Prime Function.

Exploring Your Gut Brain Prime Functions

This section explores how your Client is building their world at the level of the gut and in what ways they may be limiting themselves with gut brain Prime Functions. This provides you and the Client with avenues to expand and evolve their gut intelligence to embrace greater skills in the Prime Functions of the gut and how they are *'encouraging'* their life.

> *Mobilization: Do you have any blocks, challenges or difficulties in getting moving and taking action in any contexts of your life? Are there areas of life in which you are not easily able to motivate and mobilize yourself? Are there specific times and contexts in which you find yourself procrastinating or stalling? How could you generate more action, movement and motivation in your life?*

Movement and mobilization are necessary to achieve outcomes and create opportunities in life. People can block themselves from taking action in all sorts of creative ways (this is often how some people really express their creativity). As the great motivational speaker Zig Zigler so perspicaciously pointed out, *'Motivation follows action'*, so your Client really does need to become skilled in getting moving, taking congruent action and mobilizing themselves to do what's needed to achieve success in their life.

Your Client's response to these questions about mobilization can provide rich material for *m*BIT Coaching. Their patterns around this Prime Function will probably show up in many areas of their life. Bringing greater awareness and change to them can really create generative shifts across many contexts and ripple out into their world in manifold ways.

Self-Preservation: Are there any areas or contexts of life that you experience threat, fear or overwhelm in? What are the triggers? How does this impact your life? How could you feel more secure, more alive and more centered?

Fear and uncertainty are the negative sides to the Self-Preservation Prime Function. They can block change and growth. Used appropriately however they can become '*move away from*' motivators for change and personal evolution, especially when paired with appropriate hungers for positive change to create a '*sling shot*' effect. The flip side of this Prime Function is the aspects of action that are life affirming and truly bring your Client alive. So explore your Client's answers to these questions through a lens of how they are generating fear, threat and patterns of peril in their life.

Also note that one response to avoiding fear is to utilize apathy and lack of motivation to avoid, for example, the fear of failure. So explore any patterns they have around lack of energy, which of course should also show up in the previous item on Mobilization. As you uncover areas, triggers and contexts in which the Client does fearing, work with them to explore the secondary gains and the outcomes each brain is after in the patterns of responding, and install pattern-interrupts to these old patterns, replacing them with aligned and wiser responses that bring forth Courage, Compassion and Creativity in the Client's world.

Core Identity: Are there any areas or contexts of life in which you don't deeply feel you truly embody your self and who you are? Are there behaviors, thoughts or feelings that you do that don't match who you are deep down and you'd like to change? Are there behaviors, thoughts and feelings that you don't do that you wish you would and that are more aligned with your core-self? Is there some aspect of your core-self that you'd like to improve, that you'd like to make even more awesome? Is there some part of you that you'd like to accept more fully? What would

be a sense of self that would truly inspire you deeply?

As you'd expect, this is an area for deep exploration that has a major impact on the Client's life. You'll probably want to return to this area a number of times to really flesh it out. This exploration should also not just be about remedial change i.e. change to fix *'broken'* issues, but instead can truly be an area for generative and transformational change. What sort of ontology (way of being, doing and becoming) would your Client like to embody? What would be their ideal and most awesome sense of self'ing? What sort of core identity do they deeply need and want to evolve in their world? What is their highest expressing of self (their Higher Self'ing) that would continue to inspire them and fill their life with deep visceral meaning and purpose? These are the areas to explore with *m*BIT Coaching with your Client.

Exploring Your Head Brain Prime Functions

This section explores how your Client is creating their world at the level of the head and in what ways they may be limiting themselves with head brain Prime Functions. This provides you and the Client with avenues to expand and evolve their head brain processing to embrace greater skills in the Prime Functions of the head and how they are '*cognizing*' their life.

> *Cognitive Perception: Are there any patterns of perceiving that don't serve you? Ways of looking at the world or ways of directing your attention that limit your happiness, peace and success?*

> One of the first steps the head brain has to do is take in the information arriving from the 5 senses (and the signals and messages coming internally from the other neural networks) and construct perceptions from this blooming confusion. We all have varied ways of perceiving the world, of deleting, generalizing and distorting the underlying sensory data. Our attention is limited and so our perceptions get directed by unconscious attentional processes.
>
> In this exercise, you want your Client to begin to be aware of their patterns of perceiving and attentional selection. This is a really important Prime Function and generative changes at this stage of head-based processing can have really wide ranging impacts on the person's *mBraining* and their life. So spend quite a bit of time exploring and making fine grained distinctions on this process with your Client.

> *Thinking: Do you have, or do, any patterns or habitual ways of thinking that don't serve you? Are you troubled by recurring thoughts that disturb you or lead to unresourceful states? Are there ways of thinking that you could improve or upgrade?*

> What you are looking for here are limiting beliefs, generalizations and complex-

equivalences, and fixed or rigid ways of thinking that impoverish your Client's world. For example, does the Client indulge in pessimistic or negative thinking patterns versus optimistic thinking patterns? If you find such patterns you can explore them with the Client using the *m*BIT Highest Expression Foundational Sequence process to emerge greater wisdom in how your Client is *'thinking their world into being'*. If you have skills in NLP, CBT (Cognitive Behavioral Therapy) or other useful cognitive modalities, you can also coach your Client in various pattern-interrupt processes to block unwanted thoughts.

Making Meaning: Are there any stories in your life that aren't serving you well? What are they? Do you have any patterns in your life where you make meaning from your experience in a way that upsets you or is dysfunctional? Are there patterns, beliefs and stories that you could improve and upgrade?

We largely make meaning through metaphor. So here you want the Client to explore the narratives and stories of their life and the underlying patterns of *'metaphoring'* they do habitually. For example, does the Client operate from a metaphor that says that *"life is a game"* and thereby they construct a reality in which there are winners and losers, arbitrary rules etc.? You cannot not do metaphoring, that's how the brain constructs meaning, however you can have choice and requisite variety, and meta-awareness about the metaphors, narratives and stories you are choosing and using to construct and make meaning of your world.

This exercise is about opening up your Client's awareness to their stories and narratives and about bringing more choice and wisdom to how they do that process. Explore with them, using *m*BIT Coaching processes, how their aligned three intelligences feel and experience the stories and metaphors they are living by. Do all the brains agree with the stories? Are there better stories they'd like to live by? Are the stories bringing wisdom to the person's life?

Exploring the Prime Function Constraints

Sometimes people use one Prime Function to do the job of another. One example we've seen was an Entertainer who used valuing of others attention in place of connecting with others. This person didn't like connecting deeply with others and didn't exercise that Prime Function, but instead used values to drive their relationship with others by performing on stage because they wanted to be adored and valued by others as a way of connecting and relating.

> *Are there any areas of your life where you use one Prime Function to do the job of another? As you look through the Prime Function list of the three brains, is there one that you might be satisfying by using one of the others in its place? If so, what are the challenges and issues that arise as a result of this? How does this impact your life?*

Heart Brain Prime Functions
- Emoting
- Relational Affect
- Values

Gut Brain Prime Functions
- Mobilization
- Self-Preservation
- Core Identity

Head Brain Prime Functions
- Cognitive Perception
- Thinking
- Making Meaning

Facilitators Guide

This is quite a difficult and challenging exercise and one you may have to work directly with your Client on, using your own deep intuitions about the Client's patterns and processes to really uncover any Prime Function Constraints. Once, and if, you have uncovered any constraints, explore them and the secondary gains they provide using *m*BIT Coaching to determine emergent and wiser ways for the Client to achieve their outcomes while building Prime Function skills that are more aligned and appropriate.

7.

Core Competencies Exploration

Each of your brains (head, heart, gut) has its own domains of expertise and core competencies that it's involved in. In *m*BIT, we have laid these competencies out in a framework that divides the competencies between the brains and across Autonomic mode. You see, the Autonomic Nervous System (ANS) innervates and influences the states and competencies that each of the brains can operate from. When you are stressed and your ANS is sympathetic dominant, you do not feel calm, you can't think clearly and your gut is often in a knot. Similarly, if you are overly depressed and in parasympathetic dominant mode, then your brains cannot function optimally either. You won't be able to think properly, your heart will be down-regulated and your gut will lack vigor and motivation.

The *m*BIT Core Competencies Framework enables you to quickly determine how each of your intelligences is functioning in relation to an issue, and what specific coherent-balanced state might be needed to function optimally and adaptively. Understanding the core competencies helps you quickly recognize how each brain is fulfilling its Prime Functions via manifested behaviors. You'll then be able to discern if those behavioral expressions are optimizing or detracting from your ability for wise living and overall wellbeing. If each or any of your brains are operating in suboptimal states, you'll know what needs to be facilitated within yourself so each brain can fulfill its Prime Function at the highest level.

In this exercise you will explore your strengths, patterns, habits and skill-gap opportunities in the core competencies of each of your brains. This will provide fruitful areas for you to work with your *m*BIT Coach to enhance your skills and bring more flexibility, freedom and choice to your world.

Facilitators Guide

Positive emotions and positive thoughts are important for physical, emotional and psychological health. Extensive research in the field of Positive Psychology over the last decade has shown that emotions and behaviors such as joy, laughter, compassion, love, appreciation, interest, contentment and connecting with others all build emotional and psychological resilience, increase physical health and help people live happier lives (for example see, Fredrickson, 2000; Tugade, Fredrickson & Feldman Barrett, 2004; and Fredrickson, 2013).

You'll notice that all these emotions and competencies fall on the '*ANS Balanced Mode*' column of the Core Competencies lists. In part, this is because these positive competencies increase cardiac vagal tone, strengthening the ability for the ANS to remain in balance. It's also because they allow the multiple brains to perform in their most adaptive zones, and to communicate and work together to bring wisdom and upward spirals of success to a person's life. In Positive Psychology this is known as the '*Broaden and Build Theory*', a term coined by researcher Dr. Barbara Fredrickson. Barbara and her colleagues have shown in hundreds of experiments that positive emotions and experiences build positive spirals of psychological functioning, increasing creativity and adaptability. As Barbara and her colleagues explain, "*Whereas negative emotions heighten one's sympathetic activity and narrow one's attention to support specific action tendencies (e.g., attack, escape), positive emotions have the potential to quell autonomic arousal generated by negative emotions and broaden one's attention, thinking, and behavioral repertoires.*"

So the idea with this Core Competencies *m*BIT Coaching exercise is to examine the core competency landscape in which your Client lives, and to guide and coach them to build more skills in doing the Balanced mode competencies. How much joy, love, compassion, generosity, appreciation, flow, peace etc. do they currently have or do in their lives? And how much more of these could they begin to do? Coach your Client to find specific contexts, triggers and strategies for increasing these positive and beneficial competencies in the various domains of their life. And explore with them pragmatic ways in which they can measure and track their progress in this. The more they focus on and live from the central column of the Core Competency Framework, the better will be their health, happiness, relationships and emotional resilience they bring to their world.

References:

Fredrickson, Barbara L., *Cultivating Positive Emotions to Optimize Health and Well-Being*, Prevention & Treatment, Volume 3, Article 0001a, posted March 7, 2000.

Fredrickson, Barbara L., *Love 2.0*, Hudson Street Press, 2013.

Tugade, Michele M., Fredrickson, Barbara L., and Barrett, Lisa Feldman, *Psychological Resilience and Positive Emotional Granularity: Examining the Benefits of Positive Emotions on Coping and Health*, Journal of Personality 72:6, December 2004.

Core Competencies - Strengths

Heart Brain - Core Competencies

Predominantly Parasympathetic	<<	Balanced/Coherent	>>	Predominantly Sympathetic
Emotional Numbness	<<	**Peace/Forgiveness**	>>	Anger
Despair	<<	**Hope**	>>	Desperation
Sadness/Sorrow	<<	**Joy**	>>	Delirious/Manic/Hysterical
Blind Trust	<<	**Trust**	>>	Distrust
Loneliness	<<	**Connection**	>>	Guarded
Emotionally Unaffected	<<	**Appreciation/Gratitude**	>>	Obligation
Uncaring/Apathy	<<	**Compassion**	>>	Vengefulness
Emotionally Disengaged	<<	**Equanimity/Emotional Security**	>>	Jealousy/Envy/Emotional Insecurity
Indifference	<<	**Love**	>>	Hate
Self-focused	<<	**Generosity**	>>	Greed/Avarice
Emotional Blindness	<<	**Emotional Truth & Wisdom**	>>	Fickle/Lying Heart Emotional Deceit
Aimlessness	<<	**Passion (Dreams/Aspirations/Values/Purpose)**	>>	Obsession

Gut Brain - Core Competencies

Predominantly Parasympathetic	<<	Balanced/Coherent	>>	Predominantly Sympathetic
Lust	<<	Hunger/Satiety	>>	Disgust
Sedation/Hibernation	<<	Action/Gut Motivation/Drive	>>	Impulsiveness
Habit/Habituation	<<	Will-Power	>>	Compulsion/Urges
Fear-Freeze/Withdrawal	<<	Courage	>>	Fear-Fight/Flight
Lethargy/Depression	<<	Relaxed/Calm	>>	Anxiety
Self Preservation	<<	Wellbeing	>>	Self Damage
"Dumb shit"	<<	Gut Intuition	>>	Gut Turmoil

Head Brain - Core Competencies

Left hemisphere (Parasympathetic)	<<	Balanced/Coherent	>>	Right hemisphere (Sympathetic)
Orienting Through Time	<<	Being Present	>>	Atemporal
Dissociation	<<	Meta Consciousness/Meta Cognition	>>	Subjective Reality
Singular Reality	<<	Balanced Perspective/Integrated View	>>	Simultaneous Multiple Realities
Mental-Efforting and Struggle	<<	Flow States	>>	Mental/Subjective Drifting
Convergent Thinking	<<	Creativity	>>	Divergent Thinking
Fixation	<<	Curiosity	>>	Mentally Scattered
Logical-Structured Learning	<<	Transformational/Generative Learning	>>	Survival/Streetwise Learning

On the frameworks listed on the previous pages, for each of the brains:

> *Mark or tick any and all of the competencies you believe or feel you are strongest in, are 'good' at, skilled in, or get the most benefit from in your life. Which of these competencies that you've ticked are your three top strengths overall? For each brain, which competency is your strongest? Which autonomic mode do your competencies sit in? Are there any discernable patterns here?*
>
> *[Note that something you are skilled or 'unconsciously competent' in may not necessarily produce positive results. This exercise is about exploring and determining the core competencies you are very skilled in, both those that you feel are positive and those that aren't so positive for your life.]*

This is about determining, at a broad-brush level, which of the core competencies are strongest and how the Client perceives they benefit (or not) from these. It's also about seeing how the competencies play out across Autonomic mode and across the three brains. You might compare the results of this with what was discovered in the Client's ANS Mode, ANS Response and Brain Preference exercises earlier in the Workbook. One of the things you are looking for here is for the Client to have as many skills and strengths in the ANS Balanced mode, and spread evenly and appropriately across the brains. This is where resilience, flow and other psychological, emotional and mental benefits arise from.

In part the idea of this exercise is to build awareness and meta-cognition within your Client about their own patterns, strengths and preferences. Explore with them where and how they use their competencies, what advantages they gain from them and also whether they over-use them and if so in what contexts. In addition, you might also explore with them whether there are any contexts or situations that they don't use these competencies and strengths in, and if so, how they might make a generative difference by bringing their Balanced mode competencies to these situations.

Core Competencies – Skill-gaps and Opportunities

Heart Brain - Core Competencies

Predominantly Parasympathetic	<<	Balanced/Coherent	>>	Predominantly Sympathetic
Emotional Numbness	<<	**Peace/Forgiveness**	>>	Anger
Despair	<<	**Hope**	>>	Desperation
Sadness/Sorrow	<<	**Joy**	>>	Delirious/Manic/Hysterical
Blind Trust	<<	**Trust**	>>	Distrust
Loneliness	<<	**Connection**	>>	Guarded
Emotionally Unaffected	<<	**Appreciation/Gratitude**	>>	Obligation
Uncaring/Apathy	<<	**Compassion**	>>	Vengefulness
Emotionally Disengaged	<<	**Equanimity/Emotional Security**	>>	Jealousy/Envy/Emotional Insecurity
Indifference	<<	**Love**	>>	Hate
Self-focused	<<	**Generosity**	>>	Greed/Avarice
Emotional Blindness	<<	**Emotional Truth & Wisdom**	>>	Fickle/Lying Heart Emotional Deceit
Aimlessness	<<	**Passion (Dreams/Aspirations/Values/Purpose)**	>>	Obsession

Gut Brain - Core Competencies

Predominantly Parasympathetic	<<	Balanced/Coherent	>>	Predominantly Sympathetic
Lust	<<	Hunger/Satiety	>>	Disgust
Sedation/Hibernation	<<	Action/Gut Motivation/Drive	>>	Impulsiveness
Habit/Habituation	<<	Will-Power	>>	Compulsion/Urges
Fear-Freeze/Withdrawal	<<	Courage	>>	Fear-Fight/Flight
Lethargy/Depression	<<	Relaxed/Calm	>>	Anxiety
Self Preservation	<<	Wellbeing	>>	Self Damage
"Dumb shit"	<<	Gut Intuition	>>	Gut Turmoil

Head Brain - Core Competencies

Left hemisphere (Parasympathetic)	<<	Balanced/Coherent	>>	Right hemisphere (Sympathetic)
Orienting Through Time	<<	Being Present	>>	Atemporal
Dissociation	<<	Meta Consciousness/Meta Cognition	>>	Subjective Reality
Singular Reality	<<	Balanced Perspective/Integrated View	>>	Simultaneous Multiple Realities
Mental-Efforting and Struggle	<<	Flow States	>>	Mental/Subjective Drifting
Convergent Thinking	<<	Creativity	>>	Divergent Thinking
Fixation	<<	Curiosity	>>	Mentally Scattered
Logical-Structured Learning	<<	Transformational/Generative Learning	>>	Survival/Streetwise Learning

On the frameworks listed on the previous pages, for each of the brains:

> *Mark or circle any and all of the competencies you believe or feel you are weakest in, have the most challenges with, or get the most problems or issues with in your life. Which of these competencies that you have circled are your three biggest challenges overall? For each brain, which competency is your most problematic? Which Autonomic mode are these competencies in? Are there any discernable patterns here?*

Similar to the last exercise, this one examines, at a broad-brush level, which of the core competencies are the most challenging for your Client, and about determining the patterns of how the competencies play out across Autonomic mode and across the three brains. As in the previous exercise, one of the key things you are looking for here is what's missing or is a skill-gap opportunity for the Client to build and utilize as many skills and strengths in the ANS Balanced mode, spread evenly and appropriately across the brains.

Alternately, if there is a competency that is sympathetic or parasympathetic over-dominant that is causing the Client issues in their life, you'll want to coach them up the *m*BIT Roadmap in ways of pattern-interrupting the undesired competency and replacing it with more generative ANS Balanced mode options.

Core Competencies - Habitual Preferences

Heart Brain - Core Competencies

Predominantly Parasympathetic	<<	Balanced/Coherent	>>	Predominantly Sympathetic
Emotional Numbness	<<	Peace/Forgiveness	>>	Anger
Despair	<<	Hope	>>	Desperation
Sadness/Sorrow	<<	Joy	>>	Delirious/Manic/Hysterical
Blind Trust	<<	Trust	>>	Distrust
Loneliness	<<	Connection	>>	Guarded
Emotionally Unaffected	<<	Appreciation/Gratitude	>>	Obligation
Uncaring/Apathy	<<	Compassion	>>	Vengefulness
Emotionally Disengaged	<<	Equanimity/Emotional Security	>>	Jealousy/Envy/Emotional Insecurity
Indifference	<<	Love	>>	Hate
Self-focused	<<	Generosity	>>	Greed/Avarice
Emotional Blindness	<<	Emotional Truth & Wisdom	>>	Fickle/Lying Heart Emotional Deceit
Aimlessness	<<	Passion (Dreams/Aspirations/Values/Purpose)	>>	Obsession

Gut Brain - Core Competencies

Predominantly Parasympathetic	<<	Balanced/Coherent	>>	Predominantly Sympathetic
Lust	<<	Hunger/Satiety	>>	Disgust
Sedation/Hibernation	<<	Action/Gut Motivation/Drive	>>	Impulsiveness
Habit/Habituation	<<	Will-Power	>>	Compulsion/Urges
Fear-Freeze/Withdrawal	<<	Courage	>>	Fear-Fight/Flight
Lethargy/Depression	<<	Relaxed/Calm	>>	Anxiety
Self Preservation	<<	Wellbeing	>>	Self Damage
"Dumb shit"	<<	Gut Intuition	>>	Gut Turmoil

Head Brain - Core Competencies

Left hemisphere (Parasympathetic)	<<	Balanced/Coherent	>>	Right hemisphere (Sympathetic)
Orienting Through Time	<<	Being Present	>>	Atemporal
Dissociation	<<	Meta Consciousness/Meta Cognition	>>	Subjective Reality
Singular Reality	<<	Balanced Perspective/Integrated View	>>	Simultaneous Multiple Realities
Mental-Efforting and Struggle	<<	Flow States	>>	Mental/Subjective Drifting
Convergent Thinking	<<	Creativity	>>	Divergent Thinking
Fixation	<<	Curiosity	>>	Mentally Scattered
Logical-Structured Learning	<<	Transformational/Generative Learning	>>	Survival/Streetwise Learning

On the frameworks listed on the previous pages, for each of the brains:

> *Mark or circle any and all of the competencies you do the most, the ones that are habitual and/or typical preferences. Which autonomic mode are these competencies in? Is there any discernable pattern here? How do these patterns serve you or create issues for you? How do these patterns compare to those you marked in the earlier Strengths and Skill-gaps sections of this exercise? What insights come to mind from this?*

This exercise combines with the other two before it, to help you and the Client determine the patterns of core competency skills and use in the Client's behavioral repertoire. What are their habitual patterns and processes? Do they serve the Client? What would be more balanced and wiser core competencies for the Client to become skilled in? Does the Client have sufficient requisite variety and choice in the competencies they bring to their responses in life? These are all powerful and fruitful avenues for *m*BIT Coaching up the Roadmap.

> *What competencies are missing from the Balanced mode (center) column of your list? What competencies would you like to do more of? What would make a positive wiser difference to your life?*

This question is where you explore how the Client can bring more Balanced mode competencies to their world and their life. Explore with them what would bring their spirit alive. And what specific behaviors, actions, thoughts and feelings support the competencies selected. This has to be practical and pragmatic. It has to be doable within the context of their life. And they need to be aligned and integrated around adding in these new competencies to their behavioral repertoire. Often there's an underlying reason why they don't already do these competencies. So this can be a really generative and powerful area for *m*BIT Coaching.

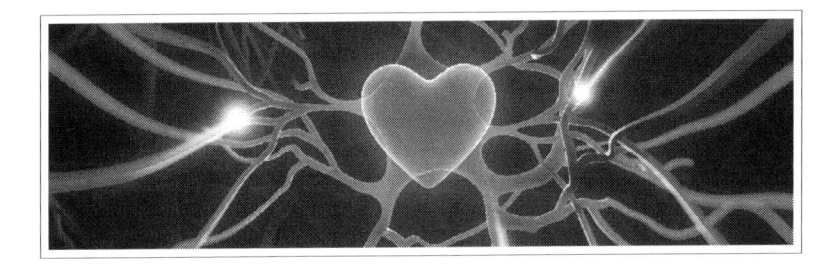

8.

Congruence and Alignment

Congruence is *'the quality or state of agreeing, matching and harmony,'* it's when all parts of you line up and are in agreement. In large measure, this is about alignment between your multiple brains. What happens when your heart passionately tells you one thing, but your gut violently disagrees? Or when your head is at odds with the messages from either your heart or gut? Have you ever found yourself fighting amongst these parts of your mind? If you have, you aren't alone. Our behavioral modeling research suggests this is an all too common experience.

The flip side of this is to eliminate any conflict between the brains, and ensure they are in agreement and supporting each other in their functions toward a common outcome. Incongruence or mismatch between the multiple brains undermines resolve, causes confusion and ultimately leads to incongruent behaviors and outcomes. You literally sabotage your own success. We've all had experiences of this, either in our own lives, or in the people around us. Think of times when you've felt torn on a decision, where one part of you has agreed but another part has not. How did that work out? Probably not as well as it could…

So for success in life you need all parts of your self, all of your brains, congruently aligned and supporting your success.

The world reflects your processes back to you

You know, it's not just about what's happening in your own multiple brains either. Incongruence within and between your brains is usually embodied and expressed (typically outside of conscious awareness) in your physical stance, your micro-muscle movements, your facial expressions and your non-verbal communication. So any incongruence you're feeling is non-verbally expressed to other people's unconscious minds and undermines your chances of success with them. This is how self-fulfilling prophecies work within human relationships. We literally express and communicate all the messages from our multiple brains, and get responses from others that recapitulate our expectations.

As an example, if someone is sending out mixed messages, you'll feel it in your gut or heart as an instinct not to trust the person. This in turn influences your own decisions and behaviors and you'll end up reflecting back that lack of trust. This can amplify in a loop of mutual distrust and cause problems in how you work or relate together.

So congruence is vital for both working with your self and with others. Success and ultimately wisdom in all your outcomes and behaviors requires alignment and congruence at every level.

Incongruence Signals

If the three brains are not in alignment or congruent with one another over an issue, any incongruence will show up as observable behavioral indicators, signs and signals. Since the brains, mind and body are connected in a Cybernetic Loop of body-mind control, what affects one, affects them all and this leads to observable signals. With sufficient sensory acuity you can see and detect these signals.

Some of the classic incongruence signals include:

- Facial expressions of distaste or grimacing
- Asymmetrical expressions or gestures
- Hunching over or closing up
- Pupil constriction and narrowing of the eyes

- Turning or leaning away
- Gut and heart reactions or feelings
- Shaking of the head as if saying '*no*'
- Holding the breath, or short shallow breaths
- Quavering or hesitant voice tonalities
- Language indicators such as metaphors or expressions indicating non-alignment

Pay attention to these signals in your life and your behavior. If you see any sign of them make sure you discuss and explore them with your *m*BIT Coach and together you can work out what's going on, gain learnings from them and get coached in integrating and aligning all parts of yourself to support your ongoing success.

Facilitators Guide

Congruence (or the competency of congruence'ing) is a core skill required for living an aligned life and for facilitation up the *m*BIT Roadmap. Your Client's patterns of congruence and incongruence will be powerful areas for leverage and *m*BIT Coaching. While the exercise in this part of the Workbook overlaps somewhat with the NIC's, Cognitive Dissonance and Trust exercises, nevertheless, this focus on congruence provides an important and useful set of additional and refined distinctions to explore in the Client's patterns and unconscious competencies.

There are two major forms of incongruence that the field of NLP has highlighted:

- Simultaneous Incongruence
- Sequential Incongruence

With simultaneous incongruence, the Client is experiencing and demonstrating incongruence across and within their multiple brains. They are sending out mixed messages and are visibly out of alignment. They are incongruent in the moment.

With sequential incongruence, on the other hand, they are fully aligned around an outcome in one moment, but at some later time, they do behaviors, thoughts or feelings that don't match the original outcome. The typical example of this is someone who wants to lose weight and goes on a diet. When they are in the state of wanting to diet and lose weight, they can be fully congruent and aligned on this outcome. But at some later time, when they are really hungry and faced with a slice of delicious chocolate cake, they *'change their mind'* and can become congruent about wanting to eat the cake. The diet is the last thing on their mind... So they are sequentially incongruent through time. In some ways, this form of incongruence reflects the nature of neural network state dependency. In one state the brains have access to particular thoughts, feelings, skills and activations. In another state, the brains operate a completely different set of activations, strategies, memories etc.

So it's important to uncover with your Client, what forms and patterns of incongruency they experience and enact in their life, and help them gain more skill and choice. Make them vitally aware of the impact of their state on their *mBraining* behaviors and teach them how to control their state management (see the exercises for this in the Toolkit Exercise section of this Workbook).

Remember, the purpose of this exercise is to bring greater conscious awareness to the Client's normally *'out-of-conscious awareness'* patterns, to then facilitate ways to pattern-interrupt the old processes, to engender compelling visions for new ways for the Client to do themselves, and finally, to facilitate emergent wisdom via coaching up the *mBIT* Roadmap so they are able to skillfully bring more congruence and alignment to their life.

Ultimately with this exercise, you are wanting your Clients to understand that life is like a mirror... it reflects back to them in results, the actions, feelings and thoughts they put into it. Life treats you the way you treat it. If you are congruent, then you'll get success from life. If you do incongruence, then you'll get incongruent results from and in your life. So help your Clients explore and understand how they are treating their life, and coach them in wiser and more generative ways to congruently transform and evolve their world.

Congruence Exploration

? *In what contexts or areas of your life do you believe you may lack congruence and alignment? Are there specific situations or people with whom you are out of harmony with or not fully aligned within your head, heart and gut about? In what contexts or situations do you do any of the following incongruence behaviors? What are the impacts of this in your life?*

- Facial expressions of distaste or grimacing
- Asymmetrical expressions or gestures
- Hunching over or closing up
- Pupil constriction and narrowing of the eyes
- Turning or leaning away
- Gut and heart reactions or feelings
- Head-based confusion or conflicting thoughts
- Shaking of the head as if saying '*no*'
- Holding the breath, or short shallow breaths
- Quavering or hesitant voice tonalities
- Language indicators such as metaphors or expressions indicating non-alignment
- Saying one thing, but doing another
- Not following through on promises and commitments

Look for patterns and triggers here. What helps the Client be/do more congruence? What hinders them? How do they do incongruence'ing? What are their underlying patterns and unconscious competencies in this? Explore this through *m*BIT Coaching up the Roadmap. Notice whether the triggers are ones that influence ANS Mode, and whether they are predominantly heart-based, gut-based, or mostly triggered by head-based processes. Does the Client kick into stress (sympathetic dominance) or depression (parasympathetic dominance) in these situations or contexts and this links with or creates the incongruence reactions? What are the stories and anchors associated with how the Client limits or stops themselves from being congruent in these situations? Do they limit themselves by dissociating from their experience? Do they become too involved in their story, too associated, and this leads to emotional reactions, meta-stable ANS shifts, and incongruence in their mind-body loop? Are there any overall patterns in this in their life, or across the contexts in which they aren't congruent and aligned?

> *What could you do to bring more congruence and alignment to your thoughts, feelings, actions, behaviors, decisions and ways of being etc.? How can you become more aware of your incongruence signals and triggers? How can you support yourself to be even more wisely congruent and aligned, and to bring more Compassion, Creativity and Courage to being at one with yourself?*

This is an extension of the previous exercise, but flips it around to focus on ways of doing wiser and more aligned congruence. The more you can get your Client to create distinctions around this, to list out specific strategies, ideas and context specific behaviors, the better they will be served in evolving this very important competency. Also note that one of the key skills needed for congruence is courage – people often allow fear and uncertainty to undermine their resolve and take them off track in their life. So coach your Client in tapping into their Highest Expressions and deeply integrate around bringing wise courage to their life and especially to those situations in which they have previously done incongruence.

> *What would a more congruent and aligned you be like? What would this feel like? What will you do differently? What specific actions will a more congruent you take in life, and how will this make a difference for you and others?*

This exercise is about bringing congruence as a value and a *'way of being and doing'* into the Client's awareness by focusing the Client on this, both at an identity level and through specific ongoing behavioral actions. It's about both *'being'* and *'doing'*; identity as well as aligned action. The idea is to integrate and help them evolve their neural networks by specific actions linked to identity. You also want to coach them in associating deeply into congruence through their Highest Expression of self (through the ontology of compassion, creativity and courage). The more your Client experiences a deep sense of being a congruent, aligned and harmonious person, along with the appropriate thoughts and feelings that match this, and ongoing actions that support this, the more they will embody and evolve the neural patterns and circuits for this in their life.

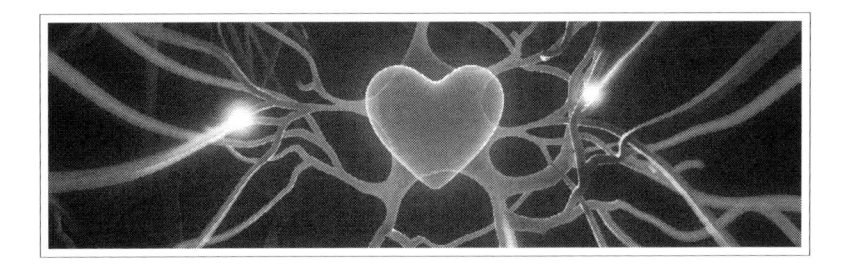

9.

Highest Expressions

Highest Expressions are the most adaptive and generative virtues or competencies of each of your brains. The highest expression of the heart brain is Compassion, for the gut brain it is Courage and for the head it's Creativity.

In this section of the Workbook you will explore each of these Highest Expressions, looking for patterns and behaviors that limit you or hold you back in truly living and embodying these competencies. Each of us has differing strengths and patterns or preferences in how we use our brains. By understanding more about your own behavioral patterns and tendencies, you can work with your *m*BIT Coach to strengthen the areas in which you have weaknesses, blind-spots or dysfunctional patterns. And most importantly, focus on improving those areas that may be holding you back from truly becoming all that you can be and do in your life, from becoming the Highest Expression of you!

Facilitators Guide

One of the most powerful components and fundamental insights of *m*BIT is the Highest Expressions. Truly living every moment through Compassion, Creativity and Courage (and in that sequence) can make a pivotal and potent difference to a person's life. So this section is designed to explore your Client's skills in the competencies of Compassion, Creativity and Courage. What are their strengths and weaknesses in these skills? What are the complex equivalences and reference structures they have for Compassion, Creativity and Courage?

Some people have had very little life experience in these virtues. Imagine for example, if you'd grown up in a family of fear and violence, you are unlikely to have received finely nuanced experiences in compassion, kindness and deep empathy. You may also not have learned appropriate and useful skills in generative courage. This would be very different if you'd grown up in an environment filled with role models and daily examples of loving kindness, deep compassion and altruistic philanthropy and giving.

So in this section you are working to expand, flesh out and more finely nuance your Client's understanding of the Highest Expressions. You might also use the findings from this exercise to do generative tasking of the Client on an area of their Highest Expression weaknesses. For instance, if they are not particularly skilled in courage, then you could task them to do exercises outside of the coaching session that require increasing levels of courage to complete. This might involve something like getting them to do public speaking, to stand on a City corner and hand out flowers to random passers-by, to go swimming early in the morning in a cold pool – things that would take guts and courage for them to do. Ideally, these generative tasks would link between and across the Highest Expressions, for example the handing out flowers in a public place has a sense of connecting with others and giving to others, and is a novel and creative way to stretch themselves etc.

Highest Expression Strengths

On a scale of 0 to 5, where 0 is no skill whatsoever and 5 represents the most skill you can imagine, rate yourself in how well you are able to do each of the Highest Expressions.

This is about determining, at a broad-brush level, which of the Highest Expressions is strongest and what the Client perceives their levels of skills are in each. You can also get the Client to revisit this exercise once the subsequent more detailed exercises have been completed, to see if their perceptions have changed.

Compassion (place a circle or X below to rate your level of skill and competence)

(No Skill) **0** - - - - - **1** - - - - - **2** - - - - - **3** - - - - - **4** - - - - - **5** (Magnificent Skill)

Creativity (place a circle or X below to rate your level of skill and competence)

(No Skill) **0** - - - - - **1** - - - - - **2** - - - - - **3** - - - - - **4** - - - - - **5** (Magnificent Skill)

Courage (place a circle or X below to rate your level of skill and competence)

(No Skill) **0** - - - - - **1** - - - - - **2** - - - - - **3** - - - - - **4** - - - - - **5** (Magnificent Skill)

Note which of the Highest Expressions you are strongest in and weakest in?

Now in the following sections, explore questions about each of the Highest Expressions in detail.

Compassion Exploration

What are the components and skills of compassion? Do a mindmap of these.

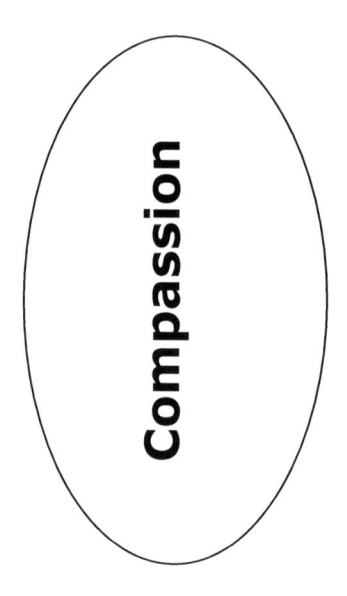

Compassion

Facilitators Guide: **Compassion**

The following are some of the key components and skills of compassion:

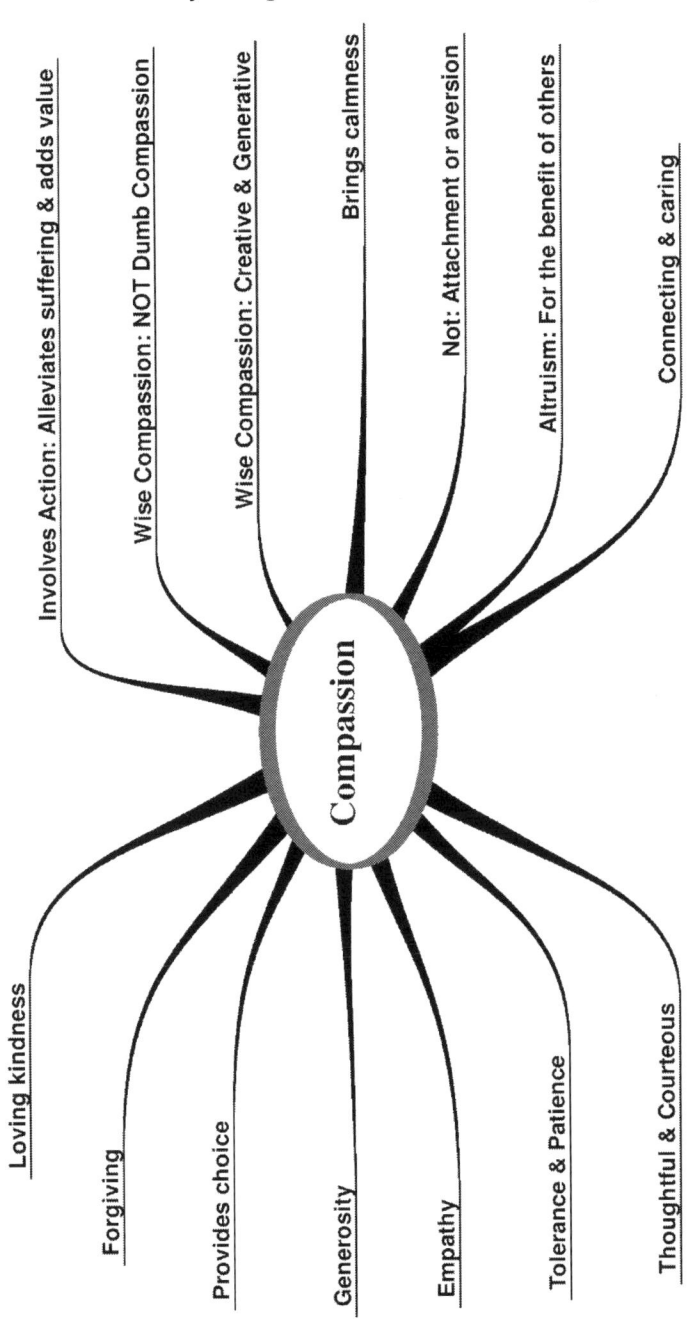

Compassion

- Involves Action: Alleviates suffering & adds value
- Wise Compassion: NOT Dumb Compassion
- Wise Compassion: Creative & Generative
- Brings calmness
- Not: Attachment or aversion
- Altruism: For the benefit of others
- Connecting & caring
- Loving kindness
- Forgiving
- Provides choice
- Generosity
- Empathy
- Tolerance & Patience
- Thoughtful & Courteous

Compare your Client's mindmap with that provided here. Are there any major elements missing in their notions and understandings of compassion? As an *m*BIT Coach you want to facilitate and skill your Client in living from compassion as a way of being, doing and becoming. It's not just about feeling the emotion of compassion and loving kindness. Though to congruently '*be*' and do compassion'ing you need to feel deeply the emotions of compassion, empathy and loving kindness, while taking actions to alleviate the suffering and add value to people's lives. Doing an action, while not congruently feeling the appropriate emotion, is likely to undermine the outcome in subtle ways.

Ultimately what you are after is assisting your Client to build new and strengthened neural circuits of compassion so that they evolve the levels of compassion'ing in their lives and their world. As much as possible you want your Client to value compassion and you want them to operate from a filter of compassion, asking themselves in every waking moment and with every decision (micro and macro) they make, "*What is the most Compassionate, Creative and Courageous thing I could do now in this moment and situation?*"

Certainly you need your Client to understand the difference between sympathy, empathy and compassion. They need to know about Wise Compassion versus Dumb Compassion. They have to understand the importance of calmness to compassion and the other supportive virtues such as generosity of spirit, joy in sharing with others, tolerance and patience, caring and concern, and the sense that we are all connected together.

The *m*BIT Operating Strategy for Compassion

While on an extended Tibetan Buddhist Meditation Retreat, after many days of meditating on compassion and practicing various calm-abiding meditation techniques, the High Lama asked our group, "*I know we've been exploring compassion for a number of days now, but would you like to know a profoundly simple process for bringing more wisdom and compassion to any situation?*" "*Yes,* we all replied, "*of course.*" "*Well,*" he said, "*it's very simple, just bring calmness to the situation, as wise compassion requires calmness. If you do a compassionate act while stressed, or depressed, your act may look something like compassion, but will likely and ultimately end up as 'dumb compassion' and create more problems and suffering than it solves. Compassion without calmness, is like taking a bath without water. You can take your clothes off, hop into the bath, and rub some soap all over yourself. But you won't be any cleaner, you'll be covered in dry soap flakes, you'll probably be cold, and you certainly won't have enjoyed a nice, warm, relaxing bath. But you'll have done all the behaviors of bathing. Except it will have been missing a vital and necessary ingredient – the warm water."*

"*Wow,*" I thought, "*so simple, and so obvious. Yes, compassion requires calmness.*" But over the next couple of days of meditation, as I reflected on this from an *m*BIT perspective, I realized that the operating strategy for compassion requires a bit more than this to truly bring wise compassion into being. Yes, we can't do wise compassion if we are either in a sympathetic or parasympathetic over-dominant mode. Compassion requires a Balanced ANS mode. However it also needs to bring more than just calmness to the situation. What else you might wonder? Well, here's the *m***BIT Operating Strategy for Compassion:**

Step 1: Bring calmness and balance to your own *mBraining* and neurology.

Step 2: Feeling a deep sense of loving kindness and compassion in your own heart, and operating from the Highest Expressions of Compassion, Creativity and Courage in your multiple brains, take action to bring calmness to the person and to the situation.

Step 3: Now, creatively and courageously facilitate or coach them into feeling and doing kindness and compassion for themselves and operating from their Highest Expressions of Compassion, Creativity and Courage in this situation.

Anytime you bring some calmness to a person and their situation and facilitate them to being even a bit self-compassionate, creative and courageous, you are bringing a greater level of wise compassion into being. In other words, the operating strategy for compassion, is in essence to do *m*BIT Coaching for the person so they become more adaptive and generative in their response to their situation. Even a small amount of calmness, self-compassion, creativity and courage will make a big difference and be an act of compassion that you have facilitated for that person. You'll have educated them and their neural networks in a wiser way to respond and you'll have planted the seeds of personal evolution and transformation in their life.

And this is the understanding you want to bring to your Client in how they perceive and do compassion. By teaching them this strategy, they can begin to operationalize compassion in their own life and in their actions and interactions with others. For wiser compassion, all they need to do is the simple process of bringing calmness, kindness, creativity and courage to a person or situation. And this is not all *'touchy-feely'*, this is a powerful and pragmatic strategy that even the most hard-headed senior executive could bring to their staff and direct reports. This is something that anyone, in any situation can do. Simply bring calmness, kindness, creativity and courage to a person, and this is an act of wise compassion'ing.

Distinctions to cover with your Client

The key distinctions to cover and explore with your Client about compassion are:

- Compassion involves kind-action, they must actually take action to add value to others' lives or alleviate suffering, to bring calmness and wisdom to others' lives. They can't just think about it or only feel empathy. Compassion involves action and doing.

- Compassion involves kind-feeling, you can't just be cerebral about it. Compassion as loving-kindness starts at a heart level.

- Wise compassion requires integration of head, heart and gut; your Client needs to bring as much wisdom and intelligence to their acts of compassion as possible. They need to understand the difference between dumb and wise compassion. Get them to read Chapter 6 of *mBraining* and explore the distinctions from that chapter with them.

- Compassion involves connection. Your Client needs to understand that we are all connected together in our shared humanity. They need to transcend the instinctual processes of *'ingroup / outgroup'* that cause us to become prejudiced against others. Research shows that compassion and empathy get blocked when we see others as dissimilar to ourselves (e.g. see O'Brien & Ellsworth, 2012). So work with your Client to experience and feel the connection we all have with each other and to find areas of similarity and overlap that all humans share regardless of race, color, nationality or any other arbitrary group membership.

- Compassion starts with self-compassion. We need to give ourselves love and support first and then extend that out to others. Coach your Clients to be kind with themselves.

[Reference: O'Brien, E & Ellsworth, P. C., *More than skin deep: visceral states are not projected onto dissimilar others*, Psych Sci 23:391–396, 2012.]

Compassion Exploration

♥ *In what contexts or areas of your life do you believe you may lack compassion for others? Are there specific situations or people? What are the impacts of this in your life? In what contexts or areas of your life do you easily do great compassion? What is the difference?*

Look for patterns and triggers here. What helps the Client be/do more compassion? What hinders them? Explore this through *m*BIT Coaching up the Roadmap. Notice whether the triggers are ones that influence ANS Mode. Does the Client kick into stress (sympathetic dominance) or depression (parasympathetic dominance) in these situations or contexts? Wise compassion requires calmness and ANS Balance. What are the stories and anchors associated with how the Client limits or stops themselves from doing compassion'ing in these situations?

♥ *In what contexts or areas of your life do you believe you may lack compassion for yourself? Are there specific situations that trigger this? What are the impacts of this in your life? In what contexts or areas of your life do you easily do great compassion for your self? What is the difference?*

Look for patterns and triggers here. What helps the Client be/do more compassion for themselves? What hinders them? Explore this through *m*BIT Coaching up the Roadmap.

Note that research on self-compassion (e.g. see Gilbert & McEwan et al., 2011), has found that people who are high in self-criticism often find self-compassion difficult and can experience doubt and fear with it, especially if the person comes from an abusive background or one that lacked experiences of affection and empathy. This fear of self-compassion has also been found to be strongly associated with depression, anxiety, stress and insecure attachment. So if you find that your Client has challenges with self-compassion then you may want to deeply explore any underlying fears, beliefs and processes that are connected with this. It is definitely an important and generative area for *mBIT Coaching*.

Without the ability to care for and love yourself, it is difficult to care for and do wise compassion with others. Compassion applied to others, that cannot also be equally applied to self, can lead to co-dependency and toxic forms of relating and ultimately be a self-defeating form of *'dumb compassion'*. One of the key issues you'll need to work on and overcome is any gut-based fearing of compassion that your Client does. This is likely to be deeply linked to a sense of core-self that embodies a belief about what sort of emotions the heart is safely able to experience (e.g. self caring and self love is not OK). This will involve a complex set of neural constraints and neural syntax and involve major work that may actually be outside the scope of *mBIT Coaching* and if this is the case, it is best to refer the Client on to an appropriate psychological or health-care professional. Then if you have obtained their explicit permission, you can continue coaching in association with their professional recommendations and assistance. This strategy should definitely be followed if the Client is suffering from severe depression or anxiety or other major disorders.

[Reference: Gilbert, P., McEwan, K., Matos, M. & Rivis, A., *Fears of compassion: Development of three self-report measures*, Psychology and Psychotherapy: Theory, Research and Practice, 84, 239–255, 2011.]

In what situations do you feel or experience compassion but not take action? What could you do to change that?

This is about the integration of compassion with courage. Explore this in detail with the Client. What are their patterns by which they stop themselves from integrating between heart and gut?

♥ *Are there any examples, people or contexts with which you act compassionately but it ends up being 'dumb compassion' i.e. it causes more issues and problems than you thought or felt it would?*

This is about the integration of compassion and courage with creativity. Explore this in detail with the Client. What are their patterns by which they block themselves from thinking more systemically and creatively? How can they begin to notice that their behaviors are NOT wise compassion? Work with them to gain more distinctions on the difference between wise and dumb compassion.

♥ *What could you do to bring wiser compassion to your actions, decisions and ways of being etc.? How can you bring more caring, kindness, consideration, empathy and aligned compassion to your life?*

This is an extension of the previous exercise, but flips it around to focus on ways of doing wiser compassion. The more you can get your Client to create distinctions around this, to list out specific strategies, ideas and context specific behaviors, the better they will be served in evolving this very important Highest Expression.

♥ *What would a more compassionate you be like? What would this feel like? What will you do differently? What specific actions will a more compassionate you take in life, and how will this have made a difference for you and others?*

This exercise is about bringing compassion as a *'way of being'* into the Client's awareness by focusing the Client on this, both at an identity level and through specific ongoing behavioral actions. It's about both *'being'* and *'doing'*; identity as well as aligned action. The idea is to integrate and help them evolve their neural networks by specific actions linked to identity. You also want to coach them in associating deeply into the congruent emotions of loving kindness, compassion and deep heart-based caring. The more your Client experiences a deep sense of being a compassionate person, along with the appropriate thoughts and feelings that match this, and ongoing actions that support this, the more they will embody and evolve the neural patterns and circuits for this Highest Expressing in their life and integrated through their multiple brains.

Creativity Exploration

What are the components and skills of creativity? Do a mindmap of these.

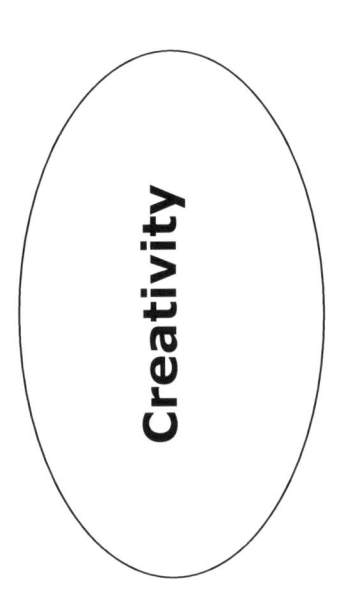

Creativity

mBIT Coaching Workbook

Facilitators Guide: Creativity

The following are some of the key components and skills of creativity:

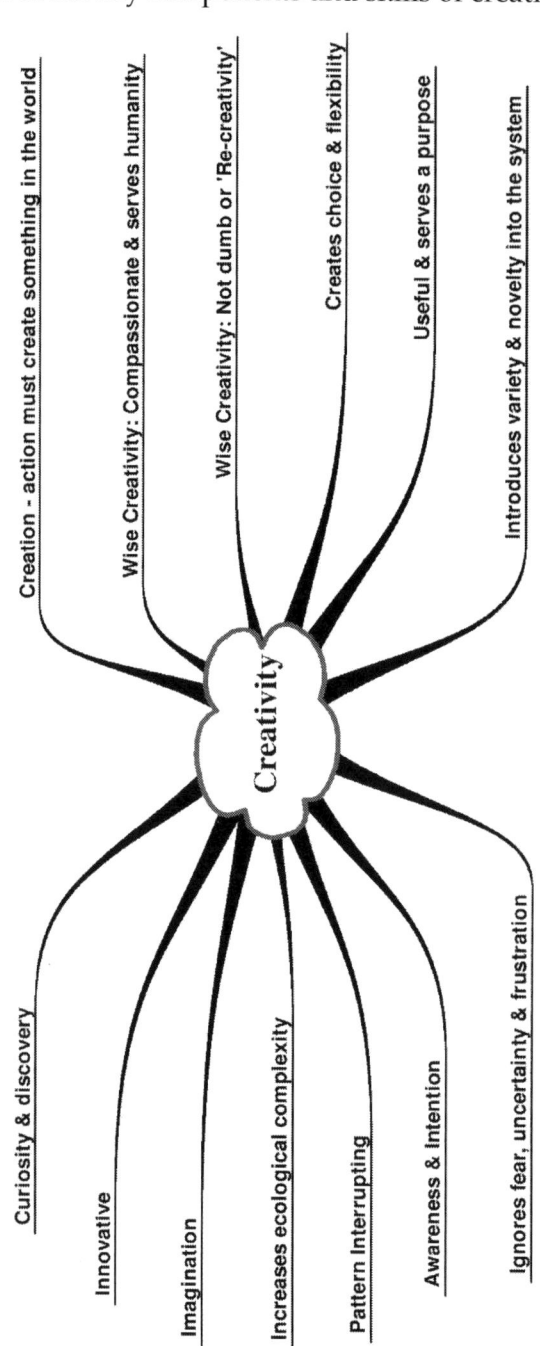

- Creation - action must create something in the world
- Wise Creativity: Compassionate & serves humanity
- Wise Creativity: Not dumb or 'Re-creativity'
- Creates choice & flexibility
- Useful & serves a purpose
- Introduces variety & novelty into the system
- Curiosity & discovery
- Innovative
- Imagination
- Increases ecological complexity
- Pattern Interrupting
- Awareness & Intention
- Ignores fear, uncertainty & frustration

126

Compare your Client's mindmap with that provided here. Are there any major elements missing in their notions and understandings of creativity? As an *m*BIT Coach you want to facilitate and skill your Client in living from creativity as a way of being, doing and becoming. It's not just about feeling creative or thinking of themselves as creative. It's about congruence between feeling, thought and action. To congruently *'be'* and do creativity you need to feel that you are creative while taking action to actually create in the world.

Humans are inherently creative beings. And in the context of a Highest Expression, creativity is not just about lateral thinking. It's not simply and purely about being artistic or innovative in what you do. While it's definitely about coming up with options and possibilities and about flexibility and curiosity, most importantly is also about how people create and experience their world and themselves. It's about how they build and construct their own subjective reality through their thoughts, perceptions and interpretations. Creativity involves being conscious of how you choose to make sense and meaning of whatever happens in your life as a generative expression of who you truly are as a person. And this is what you need to creatively explore with your Client. This is what you coach them with, helping them to deeply understand and embody this into their life.

Creativity is also about intention. What does your Client really want to create for them self in both their subjective experience and ultimately in their actions and results in the external world? Given their natural, innate abilities as a creative, conscious being, what thoughts do they want to have? How do they want to interpret whatever happens in their life? How do they want to experience and respond to whatever is happening? Coach them in the realization that they can choose, so explore with them the question, *"what thoughts do you want?"*

What you are after is having your Client understand deeply that they are the author of their own thoughts and the creator of their own meaning, which in turn (re)creates them and ultimately (re)creates and evolves their neural structures – *'the brain is a verb'*. If your Client thinks depressing thoughts, they get to feel and *'be'* depressed. If they think appreciative and happy thoughts, they get to feel appreciative and happy. Creativity as a Highest Expression is about coming from the consciousness of being at choice. Creativity is freedom. It liberates your Client from ever having to be a victim of whatever happens or has happened to them because they can always create and choose their thoughts and their interpretations of them. They can also choose their responses so that they do not compromise themselves but instead expand how they '*are*' in relation to any situation. Creativity is what enables them to be the author of their life so that you are living authentically and generatively regardless of their circumstances.

Of course, the ultimate test of creativity is creation. Did their creative process produce anything? If not, it wasn't creative, it was just imagination. So coach your Client's into this realization and into taking responsibility for their thoughts and the life they are manifesting as they (consciously or unconsciously) take action on their thoughts. Help them to behaviorally and creatively respond to the world from a more generative and higher sense of self'ing.

The key distinctions to cover and explore with your Client about creativity are:

- Creativity involves action, they must actually take action to create and evolve their world. Equally they must take responsibility for what they are already creating in their world. Thought is creative and leads to decisions and behaviors that have an impact. Even when we are not the cause of events in the world, we certainly are the creators of our responses to the events and this creates further feedback and feed-forward consequences.

- Creativity needs to be linked with and guided by compassion and loving-kindness for it to be wise creativity. Research has shown that when people are primed to think creatively they are more likely to behave dishonestly than those in a control condition (e.g. see Gino & Ariely, 2012). Whereas if people are primed for pro-social emotions such as compassion and connection they are less likely to cheat or perform unethical behaviour (e.g. see Mazar, Amir & Ariely, 2008). In addition, other research has shown that when people focus on pro-social emotions their creativity levels increase (Grant & Berry, 2011). So wise creativity truly is integrative with compassion.

- Creativity requires and is integrative with courage. According to Dr. Jack Matson, researcher and creativity expert, fear is one of the main obstacles to creativity: "*Fear is a state of mind strong enough to destroy your chances to achieve anything. It destroys imagination, discourages initiative, and wipes out enthusiasm. It quenches ambition and invites failure through inaction.*" (Matson, 2013).

- Creativity requires ANS balance, you cannot truly be creative when you are stressed or depressed. For example, when the brain is influenced by the chemicals associated with stress, it is less creative and less able to think of long-term solutions (Arnsten, 2008). In addition, research shows that creativity requires both head brain hemispheres to work together (e.g. Aziz-Zadeh, 2012) and we know that a balanced ANS mode is required for this.

- Creativity introduces variety and novelty into the system, it's about choice, requisite variety and flexibility. So coach your Client into stretching themselves and adding choice, freedom and variety into their lives to nurture their creativity.

- Creativity involves an attitude of curiosity, play and discovery, it's about *'not knowing'* rather than premature closure and certainty. Creativity uses the imagination. So coach your Client into being more playful, more imaginative and into becoming curious about what they can create and do in their life as a Highest Expression of their self.

References:

Arnsten, Amy, *The mental sketchpad: why thinking has limits*, NeuroLeadership Summit Lecture, 2008.

Aziz-Zadeh, L., Liew, S.-L. & Dandekar, F., *Exploring the Neural Correlates of Visual Creativity*, Social Cognitive and Affective Neuroscience, 2012.

Gino, Francesca & Ariely, Dan, *The Dark Side of Creativity: Original Thinkers Can Be More Dishonest*, Journal of Personality and Social Psychology, Vol. 102, No. 3, 445–459. 2012.

Grant, Adam M. & Berry, James W., *The Necessity Of Others Is The Mother Of Invention: Intrinsic And Prosocial Motivations*, Perspective Taking, And Creativity, Academy Of Management Journal, Vol. 54, No. 1, 73–96, 2011.

Matson, Jack, *Innovate or Die : A Personal Perspective on the Art of Innovation*, Amazon, 2013

Mazar, Nina, Amir, On & Ariely, Dan, *The Dishonesty of Honest People: A Theory of Self-Concept Maintenance*, Journal of Marketing Research, Vol. 45, No. 6, pp. 633-644, 2008.

Creativity Exploration

In what contexts or areas of your life do you believe you may lack positive creativity? Are there specific situations, contexts or issues in which you need to be or can become more creative in your internal and external responses? Are there contexts or situations in which you are creative but it is 'negative' creativity and you'd like to turn this around to create more positive and generative results? In what contexts or areas of your life are you magnificently creative? What is the difference?

Look for the patterns and triggers here. What helps the Client be/do more positive creativity? What hinders them? Explore this through *m*BIT Coaching up the Roadmap. Again, notice whether the triggers are ones that influence ANS mode. Does the Client kick into stress (sympathetic dominance) or depression (parasympathetic dominance) in these situations or contexts? Wise creativity requires ANS Balance so that both hemispheres of the head brain work together and one doesn't dominate the other as happens when either sympathetic or parasympathetic dominance occurs. What will help the Client get into flow? What are the stories and anchors associated with how the Client limits or stops themselves from doing creativity in their life?

Remember that we are all creative, the question is more about what we are creating and how we are creating. People who keep themselves static and *'unchanging'* for example, in the world of massive and ongoing change that we currently live in, are actually *'changing to stay the same'*. In other words they are creatively finding ways to stay the same in the face of a changing world and environment. So help your Client explore and find reference examples in their life of how they are bringing their innate creativity into play and leverage those examples through *m*BIT Coaching to build an integrated (heart, head, gut) sense of identity and value around creativity and creating. Explore with your Client how they can bring their natural playfulness into being, a sense of the *'wide eyed curiosity of the child'* into their life, the valuing of novelty and difference, and a willingness to explore and discover.

What could you do to bring more positive and wiser creativity to your thoughts, decisions, actions, and ways of being etc.? How can you bring more novelty, possibility and integrated creativity to your life?

This is an extension of the previous exercise, but flips it around to focus on ways of doing wiser creativity. The more you can get your Client to generate distinctions around this, to list out specific strategies, ideas and context specific behaviors, the better they will be served in evolving this very important Highest Expression.

In what situations do you feel or experience positive creativity but not actually take action to tangibly manifest your creative thoughts into the world? What could you do to change that?

This is about the integration of courage, motivation and gutsy action with creativity. Explore this in detail with the Client. What are their patterns by which they block themselves from taking action creatively? How can they begin to notice that their behaviors are NOT wise creativity? Work with them to gain more distinctions on the difference between wise and dumb creativity and between thinking creative thoughts and putting those into action.

What would a more creative you be like? What would this feel like? What will you do differently? What specific actions will a more creative you take in life, and what will then open up and have become possible for you and your life?

This exercise is about bringing creativity as a *'way of being'* into the Client's awareness by focusing the Client on this both at an identity level and through specific ongoing behavioral actions. It's about both *'being'* and *'doing'*; both identity and action. The idea is to integrate and help them evolve their neural networks by specific actions linked to identity. You also want to coach them in associating deeply into the congruent emotions of creativity, choice and flexibility. The more your Client experiences a deep sense of being a creative person, along with the appropriate thoughts and feelings that match this, and ongoing actions that support this, the more they will embody and evolve the neural patterns and circuits for this Highest Expressing in their life.

Courage Exploration

What are the components and skills of courage? Do a mindmap of these.

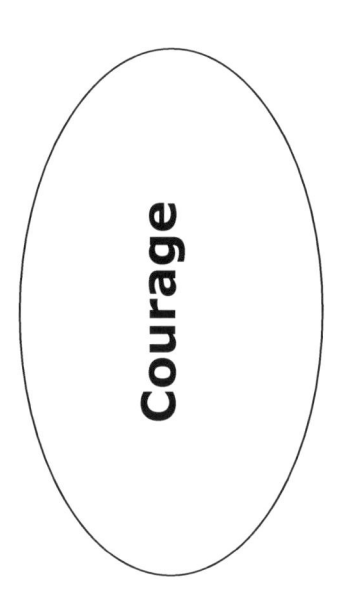

Courage

*m*BIT Coaching Workbook

Facilitators Guide: Courage

The following are some of the key components and skills of courage:

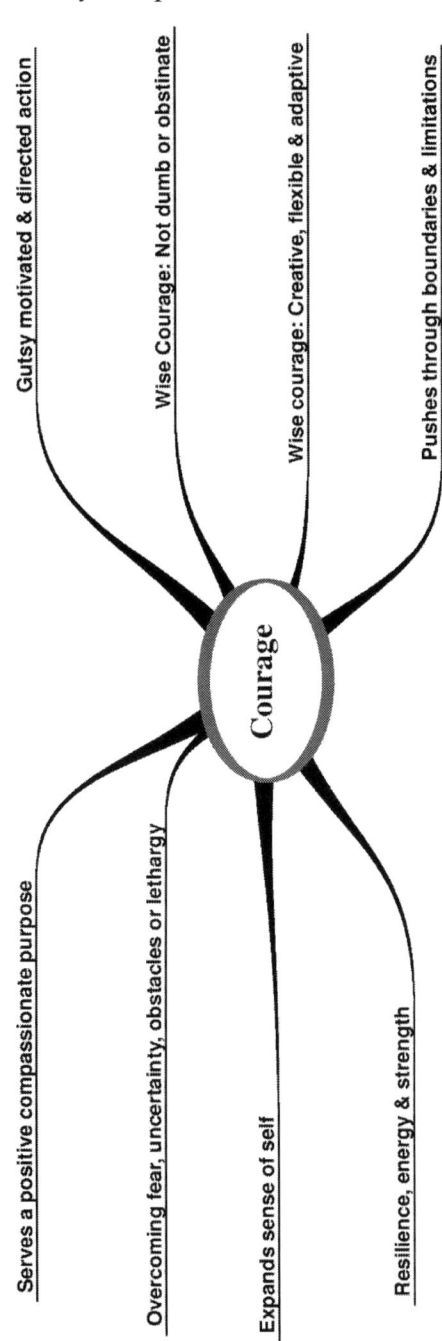

- Gutsy motivated & directed action
- Wise Courage: Not dumb or obstinate
- Wise courage: Creative, flexible & adaptive
- Pushes through boundaries & limitations
- Serves a positive compassionate purpose
- Overcoming fear, uncertainty, obstacles or lethargy
- Expands sense of self
- Resilience, energy & strength

(Courage)

Compare your Client's mindmap with that provided here. Are there any major elements missing in their notions and understandings of courage? As an *m*BIT Coach you want to facilitate and skill your Client in living from wise gutsy courage as a way of being, doing and becoming. It's not just about feeling courageous or thinking of themselves as courageous. It's about congruence between feeling, thought and action. To congruently '*be*' and do courage you need to feel that you are courageous, to believe that you are courageous and value courage while taking action to do gutsy, brave and courageous behaviors.

> *"Life shrinks or expands in proportion to one's courage."*
> Anaïs Nin

Without gutsy courage, your Client would not be able to act upon their dreams and goals. They wouldn't be able to live an authentic life as they'd be too afraid to do anything unknown, uncertain, or unfamiliar. Any action outside of what they already know would be too scary or too risky. Without courage, change from the status quo of their life would either be impossible or by accident. So you want to coach your Client to understand that if they're not able to courageously confront their fears, they'll never be able to get beyond their conditioning or author and create a more authentic and generative way of living. With courage, however, their gut brain is able to express their deepest sense of self by empowering them to act in ways that are true to the world they want to create.

Sometimes people use anger and other survival emotions to push through fear and motivate their courageous acts. While this can be useful in certain situations, it's not the most generative way to bring forth gutsy courage. Courage takes on a completely different quality when combined and integrated with the consciousness of compassion and creativity. If your Client uses anger to overcome fear and uncertainty, ask them "What does courage look like when it is not just about taking action in the face of fear, but also includes compassion for yourself and for those threatening you? And what do courageous acts look like when they are creative and wise expressions of your highest self?" Instead of coming from a reactive state that tries to compensate for fear, coach them to explore the experience of courageous action when they are in a highly coherent, balanced state of integration between all three of their brains.

Ultimately, courage is about having (doing) the guts to look deeply within and to compassionately confront conditioning and reactive ego patterns that prevent wise living. Supported by the heart and head brains, integrated courage enables the Client to create themselves anew, beyond their conditioned self. It enables them to live a creative life, one that is not defined by fear-based conditioning but one that is an authentic, generative and creative expression of who they can be at both the deepest and highest levels.

The key distinctions to cover and explore with your Client about courage are:

- Courage involves directed and intentional action, they must actually take gutsy motivated action to evolve their world. Courage pushes through boundaries, fears, lethargy and limitations.

- Courage involves an attitude of welcoming uncertainty and challenge. It thrives on overcoming problems. It also thrives on strength, energy and resilience.

- Courage links to values in the heart, it is integrative, and looks to the heart to inspire the gut to passionate action and to push through fear.

- Wise courage is creative, flexible and adaptive, it is not dumb or obstinate, it's also not a bull-dozer pushing through regardless of consequences.

- Courage serves a positive compassionate purpose, it makes a difference in the world and expands the person's sense of self.

- There are different forms of courage that relate to the interactions between the multiple brains, and people can be skillful at one aspect and not at another, so explore all of these with your Client:

    o *Physical* courage

    o *Moral* courage

    o *Emotional* courage

    o *Intellectual* courage

- Another way of looking at different aspects or forms of courage comes from courage expert, Bill Treasurer. He divides courage up into four types. Explore all of these with your Client to see what their strengths and weaknesses are in these domains:

    o   *Try* courage (initiative and bold action)

    o   *Trust* courage (vulnerability)

    o   *Tell* courage (truth/assertiveness)

    o   *Take-in* courage (ability to hear feedback)

[Reference: Treasurer, Bill, Courage Goes to Work, Berrett-Koehler, 2008.]

Courage Exploration

> *In what contexts or areas of your life do you believe you may lack courage? Are there specific situations or particular people you need to be more courageous with and for? How does this impact your life? In what contexts or areas of your life do you do incredible courage? What is the difference?*

Look for the patterns and triggers here. What helps the Client be/do more gutsy courage? What hinders them? Explore this through *m*BIT Coaching up the Roadmap. Again, notice whether the triggers are ones that influence ANS mode. Does the Client kick into stress (sympathetic dominance) or depression (parasympathetic dominance) in these situations or contexts? Wise courage requires ANS Balance so that both hemispheres of the head brain work together, so that the heart can operate from values, passion and compassion and so the gut can push through fearing. What are the stories and anchors associated with how the Client limits or stops themselves from doing gutsy courage in their life and what would be more impactful ones? What are the values and passions that would encourage the Client to move forward and embrace courage in challenging situations?

> *In what situations do you feel or experience fear but not take gutsy action? What prevents you from taking courageous action despite the fear sensations? How does this impact your life and your sense of who you are? In what situations or contexts do you push through fear and take gutsy action? What is the difference?*

This is an extension of the previous exercise, but focuses specifically on their strategies for overcoming fear. The more you can get your Client to generate distinctions around this, to list out specific strategies, ideas and context specific behaviors, the better you and they will be served in having material to do coaching with. Once you know their patterns, you can coach them in new strategies to pattern-interrupt the old strategies and instead install new ones for evolving this very important Highest Expression.

What could you do to bring wiser courage to your actions, decisions and ways of being etc.? What are the ways you have motivated yourself in the past to do courage and overcome fear (e.g. anger), but that you could now do in a wiser more generative way? How can you bring more gutsy motivated and wise courage to your life?

This is about the integration of balance, compassion and creativity with courage. Explore this in detail with the Client. What are their patterns by which they block themselves from taking courageous and wise action? How can they begin to notice that their behaviors are NOT wise courage? Work with them to gain more distinctions on the difference between wise and dumb courage and between discouraging themselves versus encouraging themselves.

What would a more courageous you be like? What would this feel like? What will you do differently? What specific actions would a more courageous you take in life, and how will your life have become different?

This exercise is about bringing courage as a *'way of being'* into the Client's awareness by focusing the Client on this both at an identity level and through specific ongoing behavioral actions. It's about both *'being'* and *'doing'*; both identity and action. The idea is to integrate and help them evolve their neural networks by specific actions linked to identity. You also want to coach them in associating deeply into the congruent emotions of gutsy courage, drive and purpose. The more your Client experiences a deep sense of being a courageous and gutsy person, along with the appropriate thoughts and feelings that match this, and ongoing actions that nurture this, the more they will embody and evolve the neural patterns and circuits for this Highest Expressing in their life.

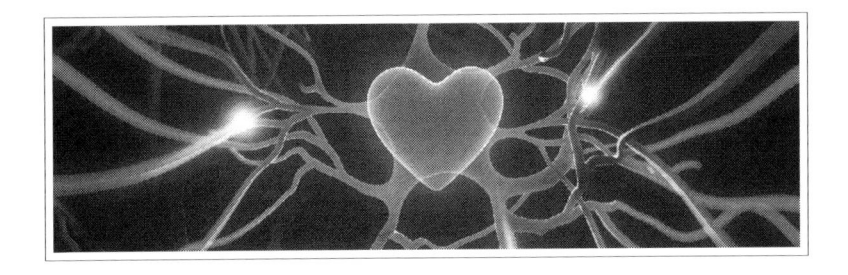

10.

Highest Expression Integration

Integrating across Prime Functions

The Highest Expressions of Compassion, Creativity and Courage are integrative, each requires the others in order to do its wisest expression. They are also integrative across the Prime Functions. For example, at the heart level, you can do joy as a competency, but you could do a form of joy that is all about your own values and emotions and doesn't take into account relational affect – a joy that is selfishly motivated and doesn't give a care for the feelings of others. So joy as a heart competency doesn't have to be integrated across all the Prime Functions of the heart brain. However, compassion as a Highest Expression is integrated across all Prime Functions. You cannot do a selfish version of wise compassion. Compassion values others, has positive feelings towards others and deeply connects you with others. In other words, compassion utilizes all of the Prime Functions of the heart in wise ways.

For true Highest Expression integration, you need all of the Highest Expressions integrated and wisely utilizing all of the Prime Functions across all of the brains. So in the case of compassion, you'd need to ensure that compassion also involves compassionate cognitive perceptions, thoughts and meaning (head brain) and compassionate motility/action, self-preservation and core identity (gut brain).

In this exercise, you'll explore how your ways of doing and living the Highest Expressions integrate across all of your brains and all of their Prime Functions. This is quite a complex exercise and may get a little confusing, so you may want to do an initial exploration of it with your *m*BIT Coach to get you started. However, the more deeply you can explore your patterns across Highest Expression integration, the more powerfully you can begin to live in a way that is adaptive, generative and integrative.

Facilitators Guide

This is quite a complex and powerful exercise. In a lot of ways it gets to the heart of the Client's identity processes. The exercise brings together the insight that Highest Expressions are integrative across the brains and across the Prime Functions of each brain. And few of us are fully integrated to begin with in this manner. This is truly where the generative power and emergent wisdom of *m*BIT Coaching shines.

What you are looking to do with this exercise is find and uncover the patterns and preferences, and equally, the blind-spots and limitations, in how the person does Compassion, Creativity and Courage across the three Prime Functions of each brain. This is a mapping exercise – An exercise of awareness and discovery. And will need strong guidance of the Client both before and after doing the exercise.

Prime Function Integration Exploration

Head: Creativity	Heart: Compassion	Gut: Courage
• Cognitive Perception	• Emoting	• Mobilization / Action
• Thinking	• Relational Affect / Connecting with Others	• Self-Preservation
• Making Meaning	• Values	• Core Identity

Looking at the chart above of the brains, their Highest Expressions and the Prime Functions of each, map or note any areas in which you feel you are not fully integrating across or between your brains and Prime Functions.

For example, you may feel you are creative in your thinking and the other head based functions, but you are not creative in how you relate and connect with others, or how you take action and mobilize in your day to day life. Or you may feel that you are very compassionate in how you deal with other people, but not in how you deal with yourself at a gut based core identity level or how you look after yourself (self-preservation).

Draw some lines around or between areas of potential weakness, points of interest or concern that you'd like to discuss with your mBIT Coach, and number them. Then write some notes below that link to the numbered items, with your thoughts, feelings and ideas.

Thoughts/Feelings/Notes/Points for Discussion:

This exercise is best performed once the Client has completed the pre-requisite exercise on the Prime Functions and the Highest Expressions earlier in the Workbook. Those exercises will provide the insight and grounding to allow the Client to uncover the more complex and deeper patterns of this exercise.

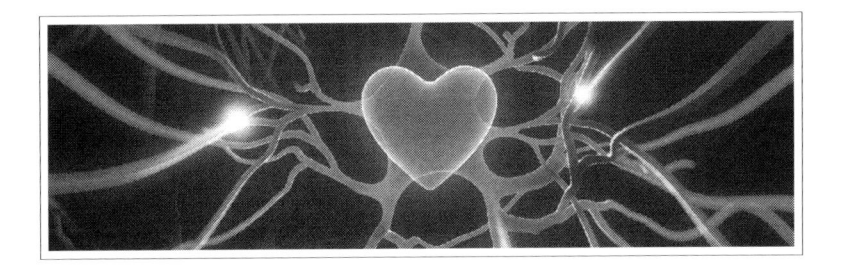

11.

Trust Patterns

"Without trust there is nothing."

If there is no trust between each of your brains then you can forget true alignment and integration. If your head doesn't trust your heart, or your heart doesn't trust your gut, the lack of trust will undermine congruence and cause blocking of messages and integration between the brains. It's really no different from how you treat someone in your own life that you distrust completely. You'll ignore or discredit the things they tell you, thinking that it's just more lies.

There is a structure to the process of trust, and in order to build trust between the brains, you need to understand that structure and find the points of failure in the process and remedy them. As you rebuild trust, only then can you fully coach the three brains into congruence, agreement and alignment.

Trust between your brains involves four key components:

- Communication
- Caring
- Consistency
- Competency

In the following exercises you will explore the patterns of trust in both your life and between your multiple brains. By becoming aware of and understanding your patterns and blocks to trusting, you can start to build more generative and wiser ways of trusting in your relationships, both within yourself and with others. This is an exceptionally fruitful area for working with your *m*BIT Coach.

Facilitators Guide

This is about determining the patterns of trust(ing) that the Client has as unconscious competencies in their life. Since patterns often generalize across contexts in neural patterning systems, you are likely to find that the patterns the Client shows in their relationships with others are similar to how they do trusting of themselves on an internal level, including the patterns of trust between their brains. This insight is reflected in the esoteric saying, "*As within, so without*". Once you've worked with the Client to bring their patterns, and the impacts of their patterns to their conscious awareness, this becomes a very fruitful and impactful area for *m*BIT coaching work and you can coach and facilitate them to bring more wisdom and generativity to their internal and external relatings.

Exploring Trust Patterns

> **?** *In what contexts or areas of your life do you experience trouble with trusting, in which you may lack trust for others, or suffer due to a lack of trust (or perhaps even over-trust)? Are there specific situations or people you have trust issues with? What are the impacts of this in your life?*

Look for patterns here. What sorts of contexts or people do they have trust issues with? What is their history with trust in relationships? What narratives or stories are they running about trust in their lives? What meaning are they making? What is their heart experience of this? What gut issues do they have with trust in their relationships? Explore this through *m*BIT Coaching up the Roadmap and especially through the Prime Functions of each of the brains. Look for the over-arching patterns that the Client brings to how they do trust with others, and of course use this to also bring a lens to how they do trusting of themselves.

> **?** *In what contexts or areas of your life do you experience trouble with trusting yourself? Are there any ways in which you lack trust for yourself, or suffer due to a lack of trust in yourself (or perhaps even over-trust)? Are there specific situations you have trust issues with? What are the impacts of this in your life?*

Again, look for patterns here. What sorts of contexts do they have trust issues with? What is their history with trust in themselves? What narratives or stories are they running about trust of self in their lives? What meaning are they making about this? What is their heart experience of this? What gut issues do they have with trust of self? Again, explore this through *m*BIT Coaching up the Roadmap and especially through the prime functions of each of the brains. Look for the over-arching patterns that the Client brings to how they do trust of self, and of course compare this to how they do trusting of others.

Do you completely trust your head? Do you fully trust your heart? Do you deeply trust your gut? If not, in what contexts or situations do you not trust one or all of your brains? What impact does this have on your life?

This question explores more specifically the Client's understanding and conscious awareness of their patterns of trust of their three brains. Use the information garnered here to uncover underlying issues and then work with these using *m*BIT Coaching to build or re-build trust between the neural networks. Remember, you'll need to establish trusted patterns of Communication, Caring, Consistency and Competency between the brains. Also explore how the patterns of relating and trusting between the brains reflects in the patterns of trust the Client has between themselves and with others.

In your relationship with your self, between your three brains or even between yourself and others, what issues do you have with:

Communication?

Caring?

Consistency?

Competency?

Use the information here to explore the components of trusting with the Client. It may be that one of these core processes is the pivotal issue or competency that is lacking and causing the breakdown of trust in their life. The more detailed awareness and mindfulness you can bring to your Client and yourself about their patterns, the more you'll be able to work with them to interrupt the old patterns and through *m*BIT Coaching install wiser and more generative patterns of trusting into their life.

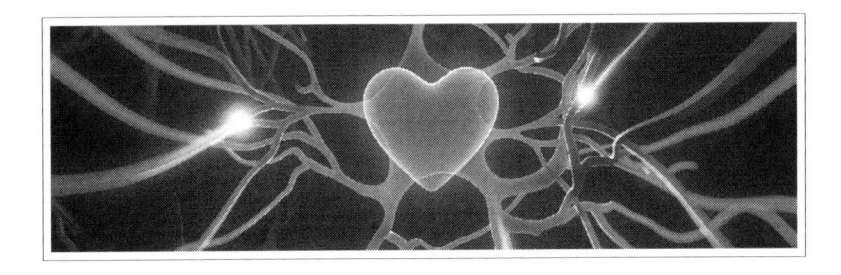

12.

Neural Integration Blocks (NIB's) Patterns

There are times while aligning your head, heart and gut brain, that one or more of your neural networks will block the process of integration. They just won't respond or allow the integration message through. We call these blocks Neural Integration Blocks (NIB's) and in our behavioral modeling work we've found a number of ways that NIB's occur. In this section, you'll explore patterns and processes of blocking that may or may not occur in your life. Note that not everyone experiences NIB's, so you may not find answers to the following exercises, however, it can be very powerful and useful to uncover those that exist, and provide fruitful areas for you to work with your *m*BIT Coach.

To give you something to work with, the following lists summarize how the brains can do blocking. For further info or details about this please refer to *mBraining* Chapter 6 or speak to your *m*BIT Coach to go through this with you.

How the heart can do NIB'ing

The heart brain can block integration through typical emotional and physical responses of:

1. Lethargy or apathy

2. Heart palpitations

3. Heart *'freak out'*

4. Emotional shut down, emotional stonewalling

5. Anger

6. Emotional defensiveness and over-sensitivity

How the gut can do NIB'ing

The gut brain predominantly blocks through the use of:

1. Armoring

2. Nausea, throwing up, pushing back, etc.

3. Scatological marking

4. Distraction (churning, dizziness, spinning, etc.)

How the head can do NIB'ing

The head brain has a huge array of blocking strategies it can use. These include:

1. Blaming

2. Justifying and rationalizing

3. Denying

4. Confusion

5. Smoke screening

6. Overwhelm

7. Going blank

8. Bolstering

9. Identification

10. Arguing for limitations

11. Insistence on not knowing ("I don't know, I don't know!")

12. Meta-commenting (explain it away, or explaining yourself right back into your current situation)

13. Double-binds

14. Quitting

Exploring Your Neural Integration Block Patterns

This section explores how your Client is generating blocks in communication or alignment between their three brains. It does this by looking for both specific instances as well as overall patterns in blocks, disconnects or disagreements between the brains. This provides you and the Client with avenues to explore the deeper reasons, messages and unmet needs of the multiple brains and provides valuable areas for ongoing *m*BIT Coaching. Note that the patterns evidenced here will often also be reflected in the NIC's exercise and Trust exercise earlier in this Workbook. So review your Client's answers from those sections to see how they fit in with what is uncovered here.

> *Do you have any situations or issues in which your head, heart and gut are typically not aligned or are refusing to connect or agree on? Are there any patterns of this that re-occur for you over time?*

This question explores your Client's understanding and conscious awareness of their patterns of alignment and blocking between their three brains. Use the information garnered here to uncover underlying issues and then work with these using *m*BIT Coaching to remove the NIB's and allow integration and communication to occur. This may require one or all of the techniques discussed in *m*Braining and that you learned in your *m*BIT Coach Certification course. Also explore how the patterns of blocking between the brains reflects and echoes in the patterns of blocking the Client has between themselves and with others.

> *Are there any contexts, people or situations that cause you to disconnect, dissociate or withdraw from? How does this impact your life?*

This question explores NIB's from a perspective of disconnections and dissociations that may indicate NIB's. Not everyone will be able to figure out NIB's directly, so this question and the following one come at the processes from another angle to help the Client uncover potential NIB's. Use the information garnered here to uncover the underlying issues and then work with these using *m*BIT Coaching to remove the NIB's and allow integration and communication to occur.

> *Are there any contexts, people or situations that are causing arguments, discomfort or disagreement between your head, heart and gut, or are having negative impacts, harmful results or unintended negative consequences and you are impacted by this at a head, heart or gut level?*

This question explores NIB's from a perspective of arguments, impasses and other *'negative'* processes that may indicate NIB's. Use the information garnered here to uncover the underlying issues and then work with these using *m*BIT Coaching to remove the NIB's and allow integration and communication to occur.

13.

Cognitive Dissonance Patterns

In 1956, Stanford University psychologist Leon Festinger heard about a group of doomsday cultists who were predicting the Earth would be destroyed by aliens at midnight on December 21st of that year. Festinger and his students decided to infiltrate the group and covertly study what happens to people when their strongly held beliefs are disproved. What he discovered lead to the powerful and informative theory of Cognitive Dissonance.

So what did happen, in the minutes and hours after midnight, when the prophesied destruction and the predicted appearance of alien spacecraft to save the faithful didn't occur? Initially there was shock and disbelief by the members of the group; many had left jobs, colleges and spouses to prepare to escape on the flying saucer supposed to rescue them. Within hours however, people began to deny they'd ever believed in the doomsday prophecy. They were saying things like "I didn't really believe it, I was just going along for the adventure." Or, "Because of our strong faith, the aliens chose to save the planet." Basically, they said and thought anything other than the truth which was that they'd been duped all along.

Based on this research and thousands of subsequent laboratory and real-world studies, Festinger posited his theory that the unconscious mind does not like '*dissonance*' and will do anything to remove it. Dissonance is the disagreeable visceral feeling we get when faced with mismatching cognitions or beliefs. Our mind likes harmony and congruence between our thoughts and beliefs and will utilize a number of unconscious strategies to remove cognitive dissonance. The tension of cognitive dissonance leads people to change either their beliefs and attitudes or their behavior.

The importance of this is that it leads people to denying reality and deleting or distorting their cognitions and perceptions. Cognitive dissonance can be incredibly damaging if it leads to denial of reality and bizarre distortions or behaviors. Of course, cognitive dissonance is like any tool or process; it can be used positively or negatively.

For example, you can use cognitive dissonance and your multiple brains' response to it to motivate and assist you in creating generative change in your life by positively aligning your thoughts, values and actions. However, when cognitive dissonance occurs outside your conscious awareness it can minimize the quality of how you experience your life and lead you into ignorance.

Cognitive Dissonance Strategies

So in summary, cognitive dissonance is an uncomfortable feeling caused by holding conflicting ideas simultaneously. It is usually felt in the gut or chest region, though it can be felt in the head as well. Typically, the tension of cognitive dissonance leads people to change either their beliefs and attitudes or their behavior through the unconscious strategies of:

1. **Avoidance** — people avoid information that is likely to lead to dissonance

2. **Distortion** — people delete and distort facts and beliefs to reduce dissonance

3. **Confirmation** — people are attracted to or perform selective bias on information that confirms or bolsters their cognitions

4. **Reassurance** — people look for reassurance from others that their cognitions and beliefs are correct and ok

5. **Re-valuation** — people change the importance of existing and new ideas, facts and cognitions to reduce dissonance

Understanding and tracking these processes is an important component of self-awareness. While cognitive dissonance often leads people into denying reality or deleting and distorting their cognitions and perceptions, it doesn't need to be that way. When you're aware that your brains don't like mismatching ideas, thoughts or beliefs, you can start to notice whenever dissonance occurs and accept it as a natural response. You can then treat it as a valid signal coming from your head, heart or gut brains alerting you about mismatch in your internal world.

The very act of valuing cognitive dissonance as an awareness tool is itself a cognition and via bolstering leads to your unconscious mind not having to automatically delete or distort the mismatching cognitions. This process allows you to gain choice and control over how you are creating your cognitive world — the world of your beliefs, values, ideas and identity. In this way you can use cognitive dissonance as a tool for positively aligning your thoughts, values and behavior.

Cognitive dissonance also relates to decision-making. Research has shown that the more effort and time invested in a decision or the forming of a belief, the larger the potential dissonance created if mismatching evidence is discovered. The more important the outcome you are working with, the more likely your unconscious mind is to perform the above dissonance removal strategies. For example, if you purchase a low cost item, you're unlikely to experience buyer's remorse. However, for an expensive item you spent a lot of time evaluating, you're more likely to experience buyer's remorse and therefore more likely to go seeking confirmation and reassurance after the purchase. Awareness of these natural and inbuilt processes puts you at choice and allows you to wisely decide how you respond to life.

Exploring Your Cognitive Dissonance Patterns

This section explores how your Client responds to (or more likely reacts to) the processes of cognitive dissonance in their life i.e. how they do cognitive dissonancing. This is an incredibly important psychological process and one of the key ways the head brain ensures that it keeps existing conditioned patterns constant. There is potentially a huge leverage for evolving your Client's world in helping them become skilled with tracking for and then responding more creatively and through conscious and aligned wise choice to situations that evoke dissonance. Learning to overcome cognitive dissonancing can make a profound difference to a person's life.

> *Think of a time when you experienced cognitive dissonance, when you were presented with facts that didn't fit your current beliefs and it created dissonance within you. What were the behavioral sensations and feelings? Thinking across a few situations of dissonance, where do you typically experience cognitive dissonance signals in your body? What are your indicators? How could you use this knowledge of your cognitive dissonance indicators to gain more choice in how you respond to dissonance?*

This question brings to your Client's awareness the (normally out of conscious) signals that indicate they are experiencing cognitive dissonance. Once they are aware of these signals they can then use them to realize in any situation that they are *'merely experiencing the natural process of cognitive dissonancing'*, and this in itself can help reduce the dissonance by the process of bolstering. So coach your Client in attending to these signals and using them as a trigger to put themselves at choice and to then go into Highest Expression and ANS Balanced mode via balanced breathing, so they can bring forth a more generative and authentic way of doing and responding.

> *In what contexts, situations or with what people do you do the following patterns of cognitive dissonance removal? Are any of these strategies more prevalent for you? How does this impact your life?*

Avoidance

Distortion

Confirmation

Reassurance

Re-valuation

This question explores the patterns and strategies your Client uses to remove cognitive dissonance. While people usually do all of the above, they tend to have patterned preferences for one or more of them. Guide and coach your Client in exploring their patterns and the impacts of those in their life and coach them in wiser and more generative choices. Also help them to note whether dissonance leads to sympathetic or parasympathetic reactions and in which of those modes they utilize which strategy. Then coach them in being able to respond through balanced ANS mode.

Reacting to dissonance rather than creatively responding through Highest Expression is not the most empowering way to live life. So coach your Client to gain more skill and choice in how they respond to cognitive dissonance and to choose wiser ways of evolving their world and neural circuits. This truly is what *m*BIT Coaching is all about.

> **?** ***What would be more useful and wiser ways to handle and overcome cognitive dissonance? What will a wiser you do in dissonant situations?***

This question links to a sense of identity around how your Client wants to ideally respond to dissonance. It allows you to coach them to become aware of new possibilities in the way they respond to and utilize cognitive dissonance. You can then work with them to install triggers for new and more generative behaviors.

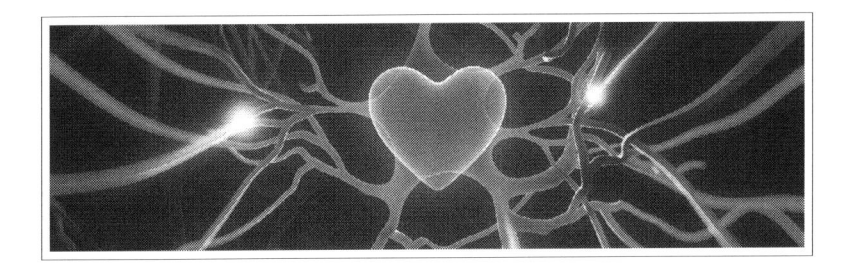

14.

*m*BIT Toolkit Category Patterns

While there are certainly many significant skill domains important for life success, from an *m*BIT perspective there are six vital areas of application most people experience some issues with at various times in their lives. Learning and applying *m*BIT processes to these domains can make a fundamental difference to the quality of your life and the results you're achieving. The *m*BIT Toolkit domains that are useful to explore are:

1. Self-awareness & Evolving your intuition

2. State management & Self-control

3. Courage, Motivation & Action-taking

4. Decision-making & Problem-solving

5. Habit control & Overcoming compulsions

6. Health & Wellbeing

Each of the domains builds on and utilizes the ones before it. Your ability for example to do courage and motivation requires skills and expertise in state management and self-control. These in turn depend upon self-awareness and deep intuition so you can tap deeply into your unconscious signals and processes that are used in state management.

So in the following exercises you'll explore your levels of perceived skills in these domains and determine your strengths, weaknesses and patterns in each of the domains. You can then work with your *m*BIT Coach to refine your skills, to align and bring greater wisdom to each of the domains and to add greater value to your life through re-patterning where appropriate.

Facilitators Guide

This section on *m*BIT Toolkit Categories is designed to explore your Client's skills and patterns in the hierarchy of domains of the Toolkit. As with earlier exercises, you are looking for preferences, strengths, weaknesses, blockages and limitations. This will show where their *mBraining* map of the world is impoverished and provides points of leverage for bringing greater flexibility, requisite variety and control to their lives.

Most importantly, as you will remember from your *m*BIT Coach Certification training, the Toolkit categories can be used as a competency hierarchy, since competencies lower on the list often require skills in the competencies higher on the list.

You can also get your Client to explore specific areas they are having challenges or issues with in their life. For example if they have patterns and problems with forgiveness in one or more of their relationships, then get them both to explore the state management and self-control section of this exercise, along with the preceding toolkit category of self-awareness. Using this as a basis, you can then coach them through the *m*BIT Forgiveness pattern from *mBraining* (and which is provided in the next section of this Workbook).

Toolkit Category Strengths

On a scale of 0 to 5, where 0 is no skill whatsoever and 5 represents the most skill you can imagine, rate yourself in how well you are able to do each of the Toolkit domains.

This is about determining, at a broad-brush level, which of the Toolkit Skills your Client is strongest in and what the Client perceives their levels of skills or preferences are with each. There are often reasons why someone is strong in some skills, yet weak in others. This can open up some deeply interesting conversations with your Client and be very fruitful areas for *m*BIT Coaching. Your aim here is to explore with the Client how they limit themselves, how they empower themselves and through *m*BIT Coaching assisting them to bring greater self awareness, wisdom and Highest Expression to all of these aspects of their life. Ultimately, it's about ensuring they are well-rounded in all of these key and vitally important categories of life skills.

Self-awareness & Intuition (place a circle or X below to rate your level of skill and competence)

(No Skill) **0** - - - - - **1** - - - - - **2** - - - - - **3** - - - - - **4** - - - - - **5** (Magnificent Skill)

State management & Self-control (place a circle or X below to rate your level of skill and competence)

(No Skill) **0** - - - - - **1** - - - - - **2** - - - - - **3** - - - - - **4** - - - - - **5** (Magnificent Skill)

Courage, Motivation & Action-taking (place a circle or X below to rate your level of skill and competence)

(No Skill) **0** - - - - - **1** - - - - - **2** - - - - - **3** - - - - - **4** - - - - - **5** (Magnificent Skill)

Decision-making & Problem-solving (place a circle or X below to rate your level of skill and competence)

(No Skill) **0 - - - - - 1 - - - - - 2 - - - - - 3 - - - - - 4 - - - - - 5** (Magnificent Skill)

Habit control & Overcoming compulsions (place a circle or X below to rate your level of skill and competence)

(No Skill) **0 - - - - - 1 - - - - - 2 - - - - - 3 - - - - - 4 - - - - - 5** (Magnificent Skill)

Health & Well-being (place a circle or X below to rate your level of skill and competence)

(No Skill) **0 - - - - - 1 - - - - - 2 - - - - - 3 - - - - - 4 - - - - - 5** (Magnificent Skill)

Self-awareness & Intuition

> *In what contexts or areas of your life do you believe you may lack self-awareness or intuition? Are there specific situations or particular people you need to be more intuitive with and for? What might you become more self-aware of? Do you trust your intuition? How does this impact your life?*

These questions explore the specific contexts that the Client may have challenges with in tapping into their deep inner intuitive knowing. The exercise also uncovers issues with trusting their intuitive abilities and their belief in themselves. This is a really important and foundational skill-set – intuitive self-awareness. Without strong connections to inner wisdom and innate intuitive intelligence, it's hard to truly learn about yourself, about the subtle signals coming from those around you and how to read the complex environments and systems we all live in.

One thing to be really aware of with this exercise is the impact of ANS mode on intuitive self-awareness. Stress and sympathetic dominance down-regulate intuitive ability and distort the messages coming from the multiple brains into fear and survival signals. While these can be valid and appropriate in survival situations, in normal life contexts, such signals are usually over-reactions and mask or swamp the real intuitive messages. Similarly, depression and parasympathetic dominance also distort intuitive messaging. So you'll have to ensure that your Client can self-calm and self-regulate their ANS mode into Balanced mode, using balanced breathing etc. and from there learn to tune into their inner wisdom and intuitive signals.

> *In what situations do you experience intuitive messages or signals from your mind and body, your head, heart or gut, but ignore them or downplay them? What prevents you from taking your intuitions seriously and acting upon them? How does this impact your life and your sense of who you are?*

Some people get intuitive signals but then downplay them or don't give them the salience they deserve. We live in a culture that has elevated the head brain over the heart and gut intelligences. So as a generalization, we have learned to ignore intuitive messages if they don't match the stories or logic in our heads. In coaching this exercise you want to deeply convince your Client that the complex, adaptive and functional neural networks in their heart and gut brains have an incredible and important level of intuitive intelligence. Build and stack a strong convincer strategy with them to really value and give salience to the messages from their multiple brains. You could even integrate the *'idea'* that their intuitive messages are deeply, truly and really important through the *m*BIT Foundational Sequence so they can align around how much they value with all their brains, the messages from each of their brains.

> *What could you do to bring more wisdom to your self-awareness and your attending to and trusting your intuitions? What difference would this make to your life?*

This is about taking intuition and self-awareness to much deeper and wiser levels. It's about opening up the ideas of wiser intuitive knowing to your Client, getting them to begin to generatively directionalize their intuition and self-awareness towards higher levels of wisdom in their life and world.

What would a more self-aware and intuitive you be like? What would this feel like? What will you do differently? What specific actions will a more aware and intuitive you take in life, and how will your life have become different from this?

Here you are aiming to link the skills of self-awareness and intuition to the Client's sense of identity and to bring this skill domain into their Highest Expression of self.

State management & Self-control

> *In what contexts or areas of your life do you believe you may lack state management and self-control? Are there specific situations or particular people you need to exert more self-control with? How does this impact your life?*

These questions explore the specific contexts that the Client may have challenges with in managing their emotional and Autonomic states and their ability to control their mind-body system (their thoughts, feelings and behaviors). Like the previous exercise on self-awareness, this is a really important and foundational skill-set. The first stage in personal mastery involves awareness of your own patterns and reactions, the next step is to guide and control your states (and your unconscious and conscious strategies) to respond optimally and with wisdom in context. Without an ability and requisite variety in state management and self-control, it's hard to produce the outcomes you desire, and it's certainly challenging to bring generative wisdom to your life if you are at the mercy of unconscious reaction patterns.

> *Are there specific situations or particular people that you have forgiveness issues with? Are there specific situations or particular people that you have challenges with staying calm around? How skillful are you at letting go of things and calm-abiding the challenges that life throws at you? How does this impact your life and your sense of who you are?*

As we uncovered in our behavioral modeling and action research on self-control and state management, some of the core skills required are the ability to do *'calm-abiding'* – to do self calming and purposely bringing your ANS under appropriate control – and also to do the process of deep forgiving, so that you can let go of hurt and perceived injustice and create more generative responses to those around you. So explore these skills with your Client and help them determine the impacts on their life and sense of self from how they do (or don't do) calm-abiding and forgiving. Then coach them in wiser and more generative ways of doing these skills and bringing them more strongly into their identity as a compassionate, creative and courageous being.

> *How mindful are you of what is happening across and within your multiple brains (head, heart, gut)? Are there specific situations or particular people that impact on your ability to remain mindful? What could you do to bring more mindfulness to your thoughts, feelings, patterns and habits?*

As with the previous question, another of the core skills required for state management and self-control is the ability to be mindful – to be 'mind-full'. And the '*mind*' is made up of more than just what is happening in the head brain. So coach and guide your Client in the practice of becoming mindful of what is happening throughout their body and throughout all their multiple brains. Get them to go '*meta*' and be able to start to notice what their thoughts, feelings, sensations, signals, communications and experiences are, and what their meta-thoughts (thoughts about their thoughts), meta-feelings (feelings about their feelings) etc. are. Help them to start to see their stories and the meaning they are making as just that, just stories and meaning that is only one way of experiencing the world. Mindfully noticing, without judgment, what is going on in their phenomenological experience. With this skill in place, and with the growing levels of self-awarenessing that it engenders, they will be much more able to take control of their state, their mind and their life.

> *What would a more self-controlled and aligned you be like? What would it feel like to have more state management skills? What will you do differently? What specific actions will a more controlled and aligned you take in life, and how will your life have become different?*

Here you are aiming to link the skills of self-control and state management to the Client's sense of identity and to bring this skill domain into their Highest Expression of self. This is also about building motivation to give this domain a focus and bring more skill and attention to what is a vitally important set of competencies.

Courage, Motivation & Action-taking

> *In what contexts or areas of your life do you believe you may lack courage, motivation or the ability to take action? How does this impact your life?*

These questions link strongly to both the Prime Functions of the gut brain as well as its Highest Expression. So in essence this exercise revisits or is an extension of the exercises on Prime Functions and Highest Expressions. However, it goes further because it explores not just courage but also the way courage links to and drives motivation and action-taking and how that plays out in the Client's life.

> *Are there specific situations or particular people that trigger you to not push forward into your courage, to lose motivation or to stop taking action and getting moving? What prevents you from taking control in these situations? How does this impact your life and your sense of who you are?*

This is about finding what undermines the Client in this skill domain – determining the unconscious strategies and patterns that they use that take away their choice, their power and their ability to respond courageously in life. Explore the particular contexts and triggers and coach your Client in pattern-interrupting the old reactions, replacing them with more generative responses. It's about getting the Client to come to ANS balance and align at Highest Expression to transcend the old learned patterns and bring more wisdom in how they motivate action in their world.

> *What could you do to bring more wisdom to how you embody courage, motivate and encourage yourself, and congruently take action to achieve your goals, dreams and (wise) desires? Are there specific behaviors, thoughts, feelings and ways of being that help you to step into your*

courage, that help motivate you fully and compel you to take action?

This is about finding what strengths the Client can call on in this skill domain – determining the anchors, triggers and strategies they already have that can be built on. Explore the particular contexts with your Client and have them practice accessing these positive response patterns so they can call on them at will.

What would a more courageous, motivated and action-oriented you be like? What would this feel like? What will you do differently? What specific actions will a more courageous, motivated and action-oriented you take in life, and how will your life have become different from this?

This is about building a compelling, enticing and motivating future for the Client, linked to their identity and to congruent and impactful *'ways of doing'*. Take what they write in this section and flesh it out in conversation with them. Really get them to come alive with this. Then run them through the *m*BIT Roadmap so that they bring their full sense of Highest Expression and the increasing generative wisdom of all three aligned intelligences to their compelling future NOW!

Decision-making & Problem-solving

Do you have any challenges with making decisions or solving problems in your life? Any behaviors around decision-making and problem-solving that don't serve you? In what contexts or areas of your life do you believe you may lack skills or abilities in decision-making and problem-solving? How does this impact your life?

These questions explore the processes, strategies, challenges and issues Client's may have with decision-making and problem-solving. Tease these out with the Client to ensure that they have uncovered any root-cause triggers. Many of the issues people face with decision-making and problem-solving come about when they get stressed or depressed, (sympathetic or parasympathetic over-dominant) and because of the impacts of ANS mode and state-dependent neural activation, their ability to tune into all of their innate intuitive wisdom disappears or becomes down-regulated and impacted.

Are there specific situations or particular people that trigger you to not be effective in making decisions or solving problems? What prevents you from doing more effective decision-making and problem-solving in these contexts? How does this impact your life and your sense of who you are?

These questions are an extension of those above. Coach your Client in gaining more awareness and more generative choice in how they bring effective decision-making and problem-solving skills and strategies to their lives and to any problematic contexts.

What can you do to bring more wisdom to how you make decisions and solve problems?

Wisdom comes from multiple perspectives. So wise decision-making requires the ability to gain more flexibility in how the Client perceives the situation, and more choice in how they can respond. Wise decision-making also requires that the Client can bring themselves to balanced ANS mode and tap into the messages and innate intuitive intelligence of all their brains. This is really about being able to self-facilitate up the mBIT Roadmap when making decisions, to communicate with and check in with each brain and make an aligned decision from Highest Expression. So coach your Client in this process and teach them this wiser and more effective strategy. Also, check if they are getting lost in their own head-based stories, and if so, coach them in going meta to their story and gaining greater perspective as they bring in further distinctions from their heart and gut brains.

> **What would a more effective decision-making and problem-solving you be like? What would this feel like? What will you do differently? What specific actions will you take in life, and how will your life have become different from this?**

This is about building a motivating set of values and a compelling identity around being a wiser decision-maker and problem-solver in life. Take what they write in this section and really get them to come alive with this. Then run them through the *m*BIT Roadmap so that they bring a full sense of Highest Expression and the increasing generative wisdom of all three aligned intelligences to their ways of being and doing with this.

Habit control & Overcoming compulsions

> *Do you have any unwanted habits or compulsions you'd like to change? Any compulsive behaviors that no longer serve you? In what contexts or areas of your life do you believe you may lack sufficient habit control or choice? How does this impact your life?*

These questions explore the compulsive patterns of your Client's life. We all have habits and compulsions, but many of these are *'positive addictions'* – habits that serve in moderation. For example, I am positively addicted to living from Highest Expression, to staying fit and healthy and to living generatively. I feel a compulsion most days to get out for a run, to meditate, to learn and add value to my life. These urges and compulsions serve me well. However, habits, compulsions and addictions that devalue your life, or damage your mind or body in some way, need to be pattern-interrupted and replaced with more generative choices.

Remember, compulsions are often unconscious patterns that Clients have learned for managing their deep inner feelings and needs. They are ways of momentarily satiating the needs and hurts of their hearts; ways to satisfy a deep hunger and ways to numb themselves from the struggles of their lives. Rather than fight compulsions and urges, behavioral modeling research shows they can be embraced as guides and healed through compassion and acceptance. One of the most powerful orientations to use with compulsions is that of curiosity, to really become curious and explorative in how to satisfy the inner needs with love and compassion.

As compulsion expert, Mary O'Malley (2004) points out, "…whenever we are compulsive, what we are really longing for is to reconnect with ourselves. We are hungry for the experience of being grounded in our bodies again so we can live from the wellspring within that connects us to wisdom, to our hearts, and to our lives." It is this disconnect between gut (hunger), heart and head that's the message and outcome of a compulsion. The compulsion is a message, a *'gift'*, and a best attempt by the Client's multiple brains to bring an out of balance system back to loving, congruent and integrated coherence.

So explore with your Client the areas in life they need to bring more skill, choice and freedom to in their habits and compulsive responses, and coach them in developing strong habit control skills and the ability to overcome negative compulsing, replacing it with more generative loving, creative responding.

[Reference: O'Malley, M., *The Gift of Our Compulsions*, New World Library, 2004.]

> **In what situations do you experience compulsions? Are there specific situations or particular people that trigger compulsive or negative habits or behaviors? What are the hidden-benefits or underlying needs that the compulsive habits and behaviors are trying to fulfill? What prevents you from controlling these unwanted reactions or behaviors? How does this impact your life and your sense of who you are?**

This exercise is about bringing more self-awareness to the Client's triggers and patterns and also to any underlying needs or secondary-gains (hidden-benefits) the compulsions or habitual behaviors are trying to fulfill. Explore these ideas with your Client and coach them in the importance of listening to and honoring the underlying needs and messages of their multiple brains, and in more generative and useful ways to satisfy these needs with love, kindness and self-compassion.

> **What can you do to bring more wisdom to how you notice and respond to compulsive desires or negative and un-useful patterns and habits?**

This is about exploring wiser choices in how the Client responds to and satisfies their urges, needs and the patterns that drive them. The more your Client can consciously articulate what specific behaviors and strategies, thoughts and feelings allow them to have choice and freedom, the more likely they'll be to have those as valued choices in their ongoing behavioral repertoire.

> *What would a more controlled and aligned you be like? What would this feel like? What will you do differently? What specific actions will a more controlled and aligned you take in life, and how will your life have become different from this?*

Here you are aiming to link the skills of choice and control to the Client's sense of identity and bring this skill domain into their Highest Expression of self. This is also about building motivation to give this domain a focus and bring more skill and attention to what is a vital set of competencies.

Health & Well-being

> *In what contexts or areas of your life do you lack, or not have optimum health and well-being? Do you have as much energy, wellness and resilience as you'd like? What thoughts, feelings or behaviors do you do that decease or impact your health and wellness? Are there specific situations, contexts or particular people that impact your health behaviors? What health and wellness patterns do you have in your life that don't serve you? How does this impact your life?*

These questions explore the health and wellness landscape of the Client's life. Without health, all else in life becomes so much more challenging. The greater the levels of wellness'ing, the more vitality, resilience and energy a person has for evolving their world. And there are no absolute limits to this, instead it is a bliss-pointing process. You can do too much immuning and end up with issues of auto-immune problems, just as you can do too little immuning and have problems with succumbing to pathogens and disease. So explore with your Client what areas they need to bring more skill and focus to their health and well-being, and then coach them in being able to do this appropriately and wisely.

> *In what situations do you experience health and wellness signals from your mind and body but ignore them or downplay them? What prevents you from taking your health and wellness seriously and acting upon it? How does this impact your life and your sense of who you are?*

This exercise links back to the first exercise on intuition and self-awareness. Our gut brain controls and links to around 70% to 80% of our immune function. Our heart is also closely linked to health and wellness. So our multiple brains are often providing information and signals about what we need to do (or not do) to create greater wellness and health. However, people often learn to ignore or override these deeply important communications. And what you ignore gets louder. So if you don't respond early, you may end up with severe health issues that you could have sorted out much more easily when the first signals arose. Explore these ideas with your Client and coach them in the importance of listening to and honoring the wise messages of their multiple brains.

> *What could you do to bring more wisdom to your health and wellness processes? What thoughts, feelings or behaviors do you do that increase or enhance your health and wellness, and bring you more vitality? How can you do more of these?*

This is about exploring wellness behaviors and strategies, about giving more salience and value to health'ing and wellness'ing. The more your Client can consciously articulate what specific behaviors and strategies, thoughts and feelings, increase vitality and wellness, the more likely they'll be to have those as valued choices in their ongoing behavioral repertoire.

And remember to help them realize the importance of positive emotions for heart health, the power of balanced breathing in controlling the ANS and thereby the state of their heart and gut, and the vital need to keep their gut microbiome (the gut flora) healthy.

> *What would a more healthy, energetic and vibrant you be like? What would this feel like? What will you do differently? What specific actions will a more healthy and vital you take in life, and how will your life have become different from this?*

Here you are aiming to link the skills of health and well-being to the Client's sense of identity and to bring this skill domain into their Highest Expression of self. This is also about building motivation to give this domain a focus and bring more skill and attention to what is a truly important and vital set of competencies.

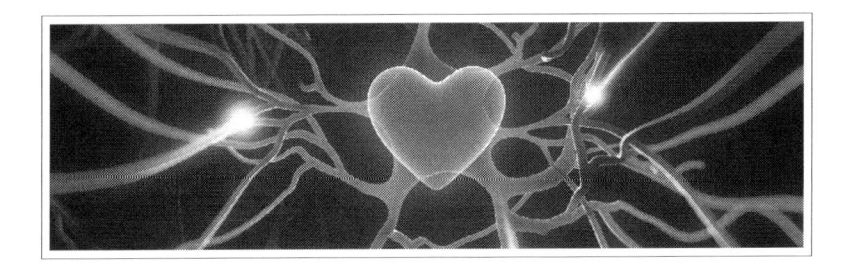

15.

mBraining Discovery Exercises

This section provides all of the Discovery Exercises from *mBraining* in one easy to locate place so that you can task your Client to complete them as and when you feel this will be beneficial. To keep this Facilitators Guide shorter, we have not repeated the text from the Exercises here, but instead have listed the titles of the Exercises with a short summary of each so you can quickly peruse them and decide if any would be particularly useful for your Client at whatever stage of their *mBraining* development they are currently at.

- **Exploring the Prime Functions**

    This exercise involves exploring and discovering the Prime Fnctions of the three brains (head, hear and gut) and how they operate in the Client's world.

- **Core Competencies Self-awareness**

    In this discovery exercise Clients learn to use the Core Competencies framework as a tool for self-awareness around how their brains are functioning in a real life context.

- **Heart Awareness**

    In this discovery exercise Clients learn to become aware of and tune into the beat of their heart to build interoceptive awareness and begin the process of more deeply connecting with their intuitive signals from their heart.

- **Balanced Breathing**

    In this exercise Clients learn to do coherent *'balanced breathing'* to put their heart and autonomic nervous system into a balanced, coherent state.

- **Amplifying With Emotions**

    In this discovery exercise Clients learn to amplify their balanced breathing by breathing and communicating positive core emotions into their heart and communicating those messages to their head and gut brains.

- **Swallowing a Smile**

    In this discovery exercise Clients learn to use swallowing to send a powerful message from their head to their gut brain. It's based on ancient Taoist teachings and works through co-innervation of the esophagus with the head, heart and enteric nervous systems.

- **Congruence**

    In this discovery exercise Clients first get into a coherent state via balanced breathing and then explore integrating their three brains' different core competencies starting with their heart brain, then up to their head brain, back down through the heart and into their gut brain, finally ending back at the heart.

This exercise works predominantly with the core competencies of passion (heart), curiosity (head), and motivated action (gut), however, you can modify this exercise to integrate any of the balanced states listed in the *m*BIT Core Competencies Framework.

- **Utilizing NIE's (Neural Integrative Engagements)**

   In this exercise Clients perform the *m*BIT Foundational Sequence adding in various NIE's to facilitate increased levels of engagement with each neural network.

- **Compassionate Self Connection**

   In this exercise, Clients learn to experience Compassion as a Highest Expression of their self.

- **Compassion for Others**

   In this exercise, Clients practice experiencing Compassion for others as a Highest Expression.

- **Embodying Courage**

   In this exercise, Clients practice embodying Courage as a Highest Expression.

- **Integrating Creativity**

   In this exercise, Clients practice integrating Creativity as a Highest Expression.

- **Highest Expressions**

   In this exercise, Clients practice integrating and experiencing all of the Highest Expressions in the Foundational Sequence.

- **Intuition**

  In this exercise Clients learn to gain insights and deeply intuitive messages from their unconscious mind and multiple brains.

- **Calm Abiding 'In joy in yourself'**

  In this exercise Clients build a deep state of calm peaceful joy within their heart, head and gut.

- **Deep Inner Forgiving**

  In this exercise Clients first get into a state of coherence, generate pure states of love and forgiveness and then apply those states deeply at a head, heart and gut level to those they need to or want to bring deep inner forgiveness to.

- **mBrain Mindfulness Meditation**

  In this exercise Clients learn to calmly direct their attention towards what's happening in their mind, body and multiple brains. This is a particularly powerful and generative form of mindfulness meditation.

- **Hungering for Success**

  In this exercise Clients build a deep visceral hunger in their gut for an intensely heart-felt goal or outcome. This exercise is about building intense motivation, a deep sense of encouragement and a passionate and congruent hunger for the success of an outcome.

- **Pushing through Fear**

  In this exercise Clients practice creatively using their head and heart to motivate their gut to push through gut-felt feelings of fear.

- **Dissolving Compulsive Urges**

    In this exercise Clients practice using their heart, head and gut to align, forgive, accept and satiate compulsive urges.

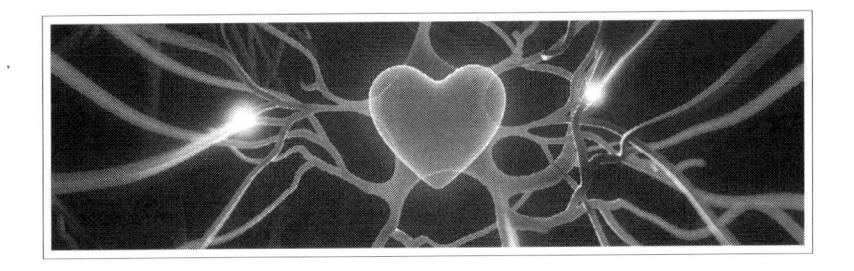

16.

Wisdom, Emergence and Personal Evolution

"Knowledge comes from but a single perspective; wisdom comes from multiple perspectives."

Gregory Bateson

According to Gregory Bateson, the great anthropologist, philosopher and systems theorist, wisdom requires multiple perspectives. In his typically thought-provoking style, Bateson was known to say "there is no inherent wisdom in only one point of reference." So wisdom requires the intelligence and intuition of all of your brains aligned together.

Wisdom also involves action and expression into the world. Wisdom that is not embodied in pragmatic action is not wisdom at all, it's merely entertaining ideas. What's more, ideas that don't guide or generate change in the world are a waste of valuable time and effort. They're more like puerile fantasies than wise ideas.

And out of wisdom and aligned action, comes personal evolution. It's about inspiring the human spirit, inspiring your self to evolve and transform your world in generative and wise ways. You can make a difference, to yourself, those you love and care for and to your world. And with neuro-genesis – the neural plasticity to evolve and change the very neural structures of your brain – you can literally evolve your consciousness and your capacity for thinking, feeling and '*being*' in new ways. So with this exercise, deeply enjoy exploring the various aspects of possibility in bringing wisdom, emergence and personal evolution to your mind and life.

Facilitators Guide

This section explores ways your Client can bring more passion, wisdom and personal evolution to their life. It starts by getting them to examine wisdom through the lens of the Prime Functions of each brain. This gets them to focus specifically on ways of growth and change, at the level of each neural network. This is followed by a more over-arching exploration of patterns of wisdom and emergence – of ways they can bring their human spirit alive and ways to flourish and evolve their world in an integrated way.

So have fun with your Client with this exercise. Get creative. Get them creative. Coach them in describing, fleshing out and embodying in rich detail what their ideal sense of self'ing can be in their life. Guide them in creating and building a compelling future, an exquisite sense of their ongoing human becoming, and in bringing that alive in their world NOW!

This exercise is also about creating a Positive Emotional Attractor (PEA) in their mind, body and life. It's designed to help them get a sense of and then step into their Highest Expression of self'ing. The more rich, dynamic and real this is for them, the more impact it will have across their multiple brains. And as you run this PEA through the *m*BIT Roadmap with them, taking them into a deeply aligned and congruent experience of their wiser, emergent self, you'll be installing a very deep reference structure for generativity.

And remember, this is NOT a one-shot deal. Don't just do this exercise once. Instead, since it's *m*BIT Coach**ing**, return many times to this exercise. Keep it alive. Keep exploring and evolving in both your coaching with them, in your own self-evolving, and in supporting their ways of emergent being and doing in their wonderful evolving world.

Wisdom through the Prime Functions of each Brain

What would be a wiser set of values for your life that would encourage you to flourish and come fully alive? What values inspire you?

For values to be wise they need to be well-formed. Therefore, the Client's values need to meet the following *'well-formedness'* criteria:

- Values must be congruent and aligned with the Client's Life Purpose and Core-Self

- Values must be ecological in all contexts of life - have no negative consequences and impacts [not illegal, not damaging to health or property, not damaging to relationships, not damaging to key life outcomes]

- Values must be sustainable

- Values must be sorted in a well-structured hierarchy

- No incongruent values in the hierarchy, the values must support and be aligned with each other

- There needs to be a balance between means and ends values

- No means values above the ends values they support in the hierarchy

- No means values at the top of the hierarchy

- Needs to be a balance between towards and away-from values

- Needs to be congruence between espoused values and operating values (values-in-action)

♥ *What would be wiser ways of feeling that would support you to come alive and live and act more fully?*

All feelings have some value and usefulness depending on context. However, many emotions and feelings can have serious impacts on health, wellness and mental stability. Conversely, there are emotions that are incredibly generative and beneficial. Joy and loving kindness for example, are incredibly protective of heart-health. They build emotional, cognitive and physical resilience, and increase creativity and problem-solving ability. The majority of the emotions that sit in the balanced ANS mode column of the Core Competencies Framework are maximally adaptive and healthy. They promote flow and bring balance to the mind-body.

Nevertheless, sometimes an emotion such as anger can be very powerful, useful and appropriate. Similarly, grief is an important emotion that should not be maligned. But habitual ways of emoting that involve sympathetic over-dominant or parasympathetic over-dominant ANS modes, are not likely to have long-term positive effects in the Client's life. So you need to guide your Client in understanding the impacts of their emotional landscape and how to have more generative choice in the emotings they do in their world. In a lot of ways, it's about learning to respond appropriately and transformationally, rather than reacting in old and unuseful patterns.

♥ *What would be wiser ways of connecting with both yourself and others that would allow you to truly live to your highest sense of self?*

How can your Client connect more deeply with themselves and with others? What ways of connecting would really bring them alive? What would this add to their life and what opportunities for growth and personal evolution would this open up? Coach them in these domains.

What would be wiser ways of thinking and making meaning that would allow you to really come alive and open your mind to new and creative possibilities?

We build our *'reality tunnel'* through our patterns of thinking and making meaning. This then either limits us or opens us up to new possibilities, growth and learning. The choice is ours. We are condemned to freedom! You cannot not choose! So coach your Client in ways of thinking that help them expand their world, of being open to learning and open to opportunity to see things differently. Also coach them in meta-cognition skills, in ways of going *'meta'* to their own stories, their thoughts and their patterns of thinking and thinking about thinking. And explore their beliefs, coaching them in re-evaluating and questioning those that don't truly serve them.

What would be wiser ways of perceiving that would help you experience your world in more generative ways?

Our perceptions become our reality. Our map becomes our territory. Our maps and perceptions can limit us or free us. Do we perceive opportunity or threat? Guide your Client in ways of perceiving that bring them alive, that give them choice and allow them to flourish. Help them to understand that perceptions are not fixed, they are inherently creative, and we can choose how to perceive and thereby how ultimately to respond more wisely.

What would be wiser ways of deeply experiencing your core-self that would allow you to live more fully?

Your core visceral self defines you in so many ways. It determines what you'll feel, how you'll react, what you'll take onboard and what you'll reject. So having a core sense of self that is strong, flexible, compassionate, courageous and creative is really vital for living a wise life. Core-self is deeply embodied. So guide your

Client in deeply integrating a sense of core-self that serves them, that inspires them, that they feel deeply satiated and satisfied with. Ultimately, your relationship with your core-self is what drives your life. If you are comfortable in your own skin and deeply happy with your self, then you'll be likely to live a wiser and happier life.

What would be wiser ways of acting and moving in the world that would deeply support you to make the most of your life?

How does your Client move through their world? What are their patterns of motility? Are they tentative and halting, lethargic and slow, or filled with energy, motivation, drive and courageous action? Coach them in embodying wiser ways of motivating and moving themselves through their life.

What would be wiser ways of self-preservation and setting boundaries, of responding to perceived threats, and ways of doing gutsy courage, that would allow you to generate a life you deeply and truly need to live to express your highest self?

Safety and self-preservation is important. But being over-cautious or hyper-vigilant is not generative or useful. Sometimes we learn (often without even realizing it) deep gut-level patterns from our childhoods, from parents and from significant life events, but that are no longer appropriate for adult levels of life-skills. Coach your Client in understanding their risk-reward strategies and developing ecological and balanced ways of responding to threats and setting boundaries. The more (wise) courage they can bring to their life, the more they can push through fear and assert themselves in their world, the more they can get out of life.

Looking at what you written above, what ideas come up for you about what would be a wiser and more generative way to truly evolve your self and your world? What would make a difference to your world? How can you live so that you are living a wiser and more compelling life?

This integration question is about bringing all of the above together. Guide your Client in exploring this deeply. Get them to do it by coaching them up the *m*BIT Roadmap. What does their heart truly feel? What does their gut deeply need? And what does their head really think is the answer to these questions? And how does this change when coming from Highest Expression?

Bringing your Human Spirit alive - flourishing and evolving

What makes your heart sing and come alive? What passions and dreams bring your spirit alive? What are your compassionate and inspiring hopes, personal visions and aspirations you hold in your heart for your life?

This is about getting to the heart of the Client's life. Coach them to inspire themselves, to dream BIG dreams, to articulate compelling personal visions and aspirations. If they knew they couldn't fail, what would they want to do in life? With all their brains and wisdom aligned through Highest Expression, what do they want to do and make of their incredible time on this planet? What is their deep and true mission?

What makes your brain light up? What creative ideas and thoughts capture your attention and bring your mind fully alive?

What brings your Client's head brain alive? What thoughts and ideas truly make their synapses zing? What's their *'Great Idea'* for their life? What do they want to be known for and know about in their world? (And note that these don't have to be global level ideas, they can relate to their own sphere of influence, their own family or neighborhood.)

What moves you deeply? What makes your gut fill with drive, motivation and courageous action? What makes your deepest sense of the courageous you come fully alive?

At their core, what moves them? What do they hunger for? What is a wise way of using their gut brain to bring more action, encouragement and power to their life?

Coach them in getting a taste of this. Coach them in digesting this fully and using its energy to motivate them in a fully aligned and wise way.

> **?** *Describe your 'ideal self' – the higher expression of your self. What is your best and most inspiring self like? Ask yourself: What is my ideal life and work? What will I be doing? What will I be creating? What will I be feeling? Where will I be? Who will I be with? What sort of person will I be? What contribution will I be making? How will I be living? How will I be evolving? Explore this in relation to your own self, your intimate and significant relationships, your family, your work and career, your wealth creating, your community, your place in the Universe.*

This integration exercise brings it all together around a representation of their sense of ongoing higher selfing. Life is a journey and not a destination. So coach your Client in reference structures for ongoing wiser emergent expressions of their self, for authoring their self'ing, across the important contexts of their life.

And help them to understand deeply, that as they live from a sense of *'ideal self'ing'*, from generative *'human becoming'*, they build new neural structures in their head, heart and gut brains. They evolve their consciousness, and bring new forms of generative wisdom and leadership to their world. And together, using the power of entrainment, we can all work together to make a profound and transformational difference.

> **?** *Looking at what you've written above, what ideas come up for you about what would be a way of being, a way of action, a way of living that will truly bring your human spirit alive, that will allow you to flourish and to live a life of true meaning and deep purpose and that will be a wiser way of living?*

This final question is about purpose and meaning. Who are you, who can you be, and what are you bringing to your life? In a sense, this deeply ontological question is at heart what *m*BIT Coaching is truly all about. So coach your Client in how they can make a profound and wise difference to their time on this planet and to all those they love and care about, including themselves.

Acknowledgements

We would like to thank and acknowledge all the people who made this publication possible.

A big thank you to all the *m*BIT Trainers and *m*BIT Coaches who undertook action research testing and trialing of the exercises in this Workbook, and all those kind and generous Clients who piloted the exercises in their *m*BIT Coaching sessions. And in particular a special thank you to Fiona Soosalu, Dr. Suzanne Henwood, David McCombe and Pauline Wong for their brilliant feedback, advice and suggestions. Without everyone's wonderful support, connection and interest this *m*BIT Coaching Workbook wouldn't be as grounded and integrated as you all helped us make it.

We'd also like to thank the following authors and researchers for their very kind permission to quote or reference their excellent work: Prof. Eugene Gendlin, Gavin de Becker, Joy Ainley, Stephen Elliot, The Institute of HeartMath, Mantak Chia, Will Scully, Mary O'Malley and Ken Marslew. And we'd also like to acknowledge that Coherent Breathing® is a registered trademark of Coherence LLC and that HeartMath® is a registered trademark of the Institute of HeartMath.

We'd really like to share our appreciation and special thanks to Sebastian Kaulitzki of SciePro.com and Alyssa and Murray Finlay of Artifact Design Group for all their fantastic art and graphics design work.

Lastly and most importantly, from deep in our hearts we'd like to thank the beautiful and wonderful ladies in our lives. Fiona, Cherie, Karis and Sachi, your love, support and encouragement continue to fill our lives with magic. Thank you.

Legal stuff

As indicated at the front of this publication, the authors and publisher have used their best efforts in preparing this book. This publication contains exercises, ideas, opinions, tips and techniques for improving wisdom and human performance. The materials are intended to provide helpful and useful material on the subjects addressed in the publication. The publisher and authors do *not* provide or purport to provide you with any medical, health, psychological or professional advice or service or any other personal professional service. You should seek the advice of your own medical practitioner, health professional or other relevant competent professional before trying or using information, exercises or techniques described in this publication. In addition, you should always utilize the services of a trained certified *m*BIT Coach when using this Workbook or when undertaking the exercises within it, and do so under the *m*BIT Coach's guidance.

The publisher and authors, jointly and severally, make no representations or warranties with respect to the accuracy, reliability, sufficiency or completeness of the contents of this publication and specifically disclaim any implied warranties or merchantability or fitness for any particular purpose. There are no warranties which extend beyond the descriptions contained in this paragraph. The accuracy and completeness of the information provided herein and the opinions stated herein are not guarantees, nor warranties to or towards the production of any particular result, and the advice and strategies contained herein may not be suitable for every individual.

You read and use this publication with the explicit understanding that neither the publisher, nor authors shall be liable for any direct or indirect loss of profit or any other commercial damages, including but not limited to special, incidental, punitive, consequential or other damages. In reading or using any part or portion of this publication, you agree to not hold, nor attempt to hold the publisher or authors liable for any loss, liability, claim, demand, damage and all legal cost or other expenses arising whatsoever in connection with the use, misuse or inability to use the materials. In jurisdictions that exclude such limitations, liability is limited to the consideration paid by you for the right to view or use these materials, and/or the greatest extent permitted by law.

About the authors

Grant Soosalu

Grant Soosalu is the co-developer of the growing field of *m*BIT (multiple Brain Integration Techniques). *m*BIT is being hailed as a ground-breaking synthesis of the latest research in neurology and cognitive science, and a true advancement of the field of NLP.

Grant is a highly sought after international Trainer, Leadership Consultant and Executive Coach with extensive backgrounds in Organisational Change, Training and Leadership Development. He has advanced degrees and certifications in Applied Physics, Psychology, Positive Psychology, Computer Engineering and System Development. He is also a qualified Total Quality Management (TQM) Trainer, and has achieved Master Practitioner Certification in the behavioral sciences of NLP and Advanced Behavioral Modeling. More recently Grant was awarded a Graduate Coaching Diploma in the newly emerging field of Authentic Happiness Coaching.

Grant has wide ranging expertise and extensive experience in the educational sector as a Senior Lecturer, Coach, Training Developer and Facilitator. He also has extensive backgrounds in Behavioral Modeling, Business Development, Senior Technical Consulting and Project and Change Management. Grant provides coaching and mentoring to numerous CEO's and Senior Executives.

Currently, Grant is a Consultant Lecturer at a leading Australian University where he runs workshops and programs on Social Media Marketing and the applications of Positive Psychology to Conflict Resolution, Risk Management and Organizational Change. Grant also runs a successful consulting company providing services to organizations predominantly in the finance sector.

Grant has published articles and papers in International Journals, in the fields of Training, Leadership, Applied Physics, Philosophy and Neuro Linguistic Programming.

Marvin Oka

Marvin is a co-developer of the field of *m*BIT and a highly sought after international consultant and speaker specializing in leading edge behavioral change technologies and research. Recognized as a world leader and authority in his field, Marvin has built an impressive track record helping organizations with strategic, systemic and cultural change. Marvin's clients range from private enterprises to government agencies throughout the world.

Marvin's professional background is in the innovative and groundbreaking field of Behavioral Modeling. This exciting field examines various forms of human talent, ability and expertise, and then seeks to create models and methods to replicate these forms of superior performance in others. Marvin is one of only five people in the world who have been recognized by his peers with the rare title of *'Certified Master Behavioral Modeler'*. Additionally Marvin was one of the first five people to achieve the accredited status of a *'Certified NLP Master Trainer'* in the field of Neuro Linguistic Programming (NLP), and at that time was the youngest ever to have reached this level of professional competency.

Born in Honolulu, Hawaii and now living in Australia, Marvin is one of the founding Directors and is on the board of the International NLP Trainers Association (INLPTA) based in Washington, DC, with representation in over 42 countries worldwide.

References and resources

Extensive references, bibliography, suggested readings and additional resources for the work described in this publication can be found at:

www.mbraining.com

and

http://enhancingmylife.blogspot.com

Printed in Great Britain
by Amazon